PLAYING DEAD

A MEMOIR OF TERROR AND SURVIVAL

MONIQUE FAISON ROSS
with GARY M. KREBS

WILDBLUE
PRESS

WildBluePress.com

PLAYING DEAD published by:

WILDBLUE PRESS
P.O. Box 102440
Denver, Colorado 80250

ISBN 987-1-948239-33-2 Trade paperback
ISBN 987-1-948239-32-5 eBook

Interior Formatting/Book Cover Design by Elijah Toten
Author Photo by TimeFrozen Photography

PLAYING
DEAD

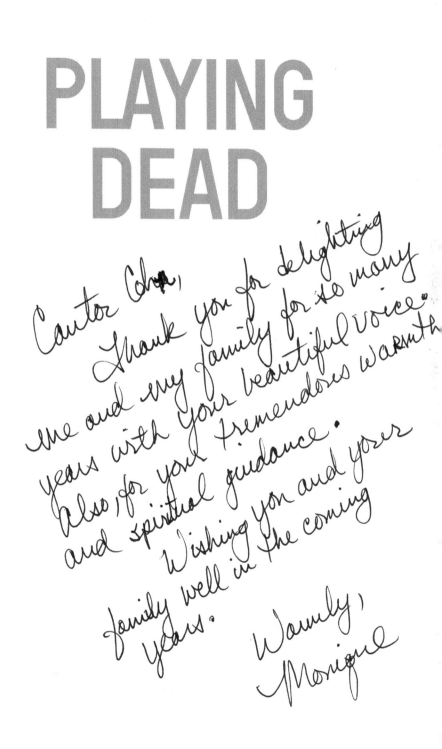

Cantor Cohn,

Thank you for delighting me and my family for so many years with your beautiful voice. Also for your tremendous warmth and spiritual guidance.

Wishing you and your family well in the coming years.

Warmly,
Monique

Dedication

To my four incredible pumpkins: Ashley, Alese, Nicholas, and Lillian.

You are the lights of my life. We have been through the unthinkable and have a true understanding of what it means to say, "tomorrow is not guaranteed."

I know it was not easy for you to give your permission for me to tell our story, but you did it anyway. I am forever grateful.

As we continue through life, at times, on shaky and unknown ground, we're always stronger, together.

I love you always.

"You gain strength, courage and confidence by every experience in which you really stop to look fear in the face. You are able to say to yourself, 'I have lived through this horror. I can take the next thing that comes along.' You must do the thing you think you cannot do."

—Eleanor Roosevelt

Acknowledgments

The author would like to thank…

Mom, for being my role model and showing me the true definition of unconditional love.

Leah, for your commitment and devotedness to the kids and me and for your daily hilarity.

Gary M. Krebs, for your patience, organized mind, and for immediately believing me and my story.

Steve Jackson and Michael Cordova, for acquiring the title at WildBlue Press.

Adam Buongiovanni and Ashley Butler, thank you for your tremendous contributions in the areas of social media expertise and production management.

Thomas Panholzer, thank you for your attention to detail and patience as my editor.

Amy Ehrlich Charney, Ph.D., for your skilled ability to cap the paranoid tornado in my mind.

Rabbi David Small, Leslie and Rabbi Yitzchok Adler, and Liora and Rabbi Avraham Kelman, for years of warm personal and familial guidance.

Patty Kells-Murphy, for your talented web mastery and tremendous patience.

Rae Tattenbaum, for having the loudest voice in urging me to share this story with others.

Attorney (now known as "The Honorable") Daniel Wilensky, for doing all that you could for my children and me and, in the end, never sending me a single bill for your countless hours of legal representation.

Attorney O. David Barksdale, for being a man of your word and obtaining justice.

Alina Bricklin-Goldstein, Marlene Geary, Lisa Lenkiewicz, Scott Selig, and Carolyn Topol, for reading the earliest manuscript and draft and providing necessary, if challenging, feedback.

Michael Neff and Marcelle Soviero, for providing professional guidance and encouragement.

The Jacksonville Police Department, for your professionalism and skilled police work.

Michael J. London, for enthusiastically getting behind this story to help market it and for encouraging me to discuss the lifelong scars that trauma leaves behind.

The Jacksonville Jewish Community, for the tremendous resources you provided to my family and me the instant we needed them.

Debbie (Deborah) Levison, for guiding me to my talented publicity team.

Jessica Rubin and Gary Schulman, for your friendship and for connecting Gary and me.

Table of Contents

Author's Note

The events recounted in this book are true. My immediate family members have been identified by their real names, and I owe them all a major debt of gratitude for their courage, support, and willingness to appear in the pages that follow.

Some names have been changed out of respect for the privacy of the individuals. A full listing of these may be found in the Epilogue of this book.

As you read my story, please keep in mind that I suffered life-threatening head injuries as a result of the attacks against me. Even under the best of circumstances a person's memory and/or perspective can become fuzzy over the years. I have tried my best to ensure accuracy and logic throughout. Even so, reconstructing the exact sequence of events and precise dialogue that occurred many years ago was quite the challenge and painful, to say the least. To this day, I remain haunted by what happened to me.

Thankfully, I retained physical copies of *everything*. In reconstructing the chain of events related to my case, I was able to refer to numerous police reports, eyewitness testimony, hospital records, photographs, and piles of other documentation. To fill in a few minor memory gaps, I conferred with several people directly involved in the story.

It is my sincere hope that my cautionary tale will serve as a wake-up call. Unfortunately, not much has changed in the world in the years since my story took place. Despite increased awareness and organizational efforts (i.e., domestic violence educational programs and agencies, the #MeTooMovement), statistics reveal that the epidemic of abuse continues:

- Nearly twenty people per minute are physically abused by an intimate partner in the United States. During one year, this equates to more than ten million women and men.

- One in four women and one in nine men have been victims of severe physical violence by an intimate partner in their lifetimes.

If you or someone you know is suffering from abuse, my heart goes out to you and your family. *Be assured that you are never alone.* There are always people out there who care and will rally to your side. It's never too early to seek counsel and assistance (though, unfortunately, sometimes it can be too late). If you or anyone you know is being threatened in any way, I encourage you to reach out to every resource at your disposal: legal, physical, emotional, mental, and even spiritual. Do not hesitate to tap into community and political resources for assistance and support, such as the National Coalition Against Domestic Violence cited in Appendix A or your local organizations.

Thank you for reading my story: It's a miracle I survived to tell it.

Chapter One

GENTLE GIANT
San Diego, CA: 1960's-Fall 1983

Let's start at the beginning with the obvious first man in my life—someone who was literally and figuratively larger than life.

My Dad, William Earl[1] Faison—best known as *Earl*—was an All-American football player at Indiana University and the Los Angeles Chargers. First-round, draft pick of the AFL, one year before the team moved to San Diego. In 1961, he won Rookie of the Year and was an all-star four years in a row as part of the Chargers' original "fearsome foursome" defensive line that ultimately won the 1963 Championship game.

At that time, in some areas of the country, black players were forced to room separately from white and often could not even dine in the same restaurants. My Dad was outspoken on racial issues and became something of an activist.

Most notably, he was embroiled in an event that became known as "the Great Walk Out" in Louisiana in January 1965. From the moment black athletes arrived at the airport earlier to play in the AFL All Star Game in New Orleans later in the week, they were subjected to a barrage of racial slurs, segregation, and physical threats. Twenty-one players,

---

1. Later in life, he changed the spelling of his name to *Earle*.

including my Dad, took a vote that resulted in their refusal to play in the All Star Game. Who can blame them? These football greats couldn't even get a "colored taxi" without being on the receiving end of taunts and abuse. In a show of camaraderie, the white players also joined in the walk out.

My Dad stood six foot, five inches and weighed 270 pounds. Despite his immense size and intimidating presence when he entered a room, he was a gentle giant—well-mannered with a certain kind of charisma. He was Hollywood handsome with skin so dark and glistening it almost looked purple and with magnificent straight white teeth. It's no wonder he was always popular with the girls.

He met my mother, Barbara Jewel Marshall, while they were attending Huntington High School, an all-black school (due to segregation) in Newport News, Virginia. My Mom, a smart, slender, outgoing beauty, loved anything she considered "glamorous." She enjoyed theater and was a majorette in high school. Though they didn't officially start dating until later when they were undergraduate students at different universities, Dad did escort Mom to her prom while she was a junior and presented her with her first orchid.

After high school, Barbara and Earl went their separate ways: he to Indiana University; she to Ohio State University. They officially started dating while he was a senior and she was a junior. After he began his pro football career and while she was still attending Ohio State, he invited her to see a professional football game in Buffalo, New York: the Chargers against the Bills. She enjoyed the game—which they won—as well as their visit, and their relationship evolved into a long-distance romance.

Months later, Dad visited her at Ohio State and surprised her with his Kappa Alpha Psi fraternity pin. Back in those days, "pinning a girl" was a big deal and signaled an engagement forthcoming—which did occur shortly thereafter. They married on June 8, 1963. They had such a large wedding that police had to direct traffic.

My Mom suffered some miscarriages in their early years, which explains why I was adopted from a San Francisco foster home in 1966, a few months after I was born. My parents had to endure a ten-hour drive from San Diego to San Francisco to get me. I'm told that I cried in my mother's arms the entire way back.

We lived in a custom-built, split-level cedar home on Laurie Lane in East San Diego, which was an up-and-coming area at that time. Most of the walls were solid oak, except for two made of plaster, upon which a local artist had painted custom murals. I don't remember much about my Dad even being in this house, since my parents separated while I was young. Once my parents were divorced, my father seemed to lack the tools necessary to maintain a relationship with me. In fact, he seemed to struggle with relationships in general.

At the same time, my mother battled alcoholism—a disease we believe was inherited from her mother's side of the family. On several occasions she would drink vodka to the point of blacking out. In social situations, she would end up so inebriated that she would become belligerent and embarrass my Dad.

As with many marriages, it was the little things that eroded their relationship, though her drinking was a contributing factor. On one occasion, she drunkenly cursed out a top bank executive at the Bali Hai Polynesian restaurant in San Diego, which was the last straw for my Dad. Proper and dignified, he could no longer tolerate her behavior and made up his mind to leave.

His first instinct was to fight for custody of me, but this was a losing battle for men at that time when it was largely believed that only women could care for young children. Also, my Dad had a demanding travel schedule, so he would have needed full time childcare. He tried to enlist the assistance of my paternal grandmother to take care of me, but she worked full time.

After the marriage ended, my Mom was engaged twice over a period of thirty years but never remarried. I suppose she never truly let go of my Dad.

***

As the years passed, my mother was left fending for herself as a single parent. Though my Dad gave her the house, the car (a Ford Thunderbird), and all our other major possessions, he was not forthcoming with financial support. He had visitation rights with me and at first followed through on them, but after a while found that the drop-offs were too emotionally painful for him, and he stopped coming.

To be honest, I don't know how my Mom managed to support us. She had a beautiful voice, so for a short time— and some extra cash—she sang Aretha Franklin's and Gladys Knight's tunes in local nightclubs. I enjoyed when her talent surfaced at home, and together we sang along to all the Motown tunes that she played on our phonograph.

I recall her suffering from depression—which was not discussed at the time—and that she spent a lot of time in bed when she wasn't shopping. Even at a young age I was aware of her drinking and remember emptying her vodka bottles and filling them with water.

My Mom was not religious, but felt I needed to attend a private school. I was taken to school daily by Mrs. Lefton—a stout blonde with wavy hair and a warm smile. The Leftons lived down the hill from us with four girls and a boy. Mrs. Lefton drove her five children and me to our small Christian school and then to church on Sundays in their large passenger van. Growing up I felt like a member of their family. At school and at church, something always seemed to prevent me from finding secure footing. Perhaps it was because my Mom never attended church with me; I was always in tow with the Leftons. For a while I tried the soulful black church in town—which seemed to help a bit.

Personal safety has always been an issue in my life. When I was about five years old, as a result of a break-in, we had to change the locks on our front door. Cliff Locke—aptly named, since he was the locksmith we hired to complete the job—was welcomed into the house by my mother, who subsequently passed out on the couch.

After completing his work, Cliff tried to wake my mother to let her know he was finished. Let's just say he wasn't exactly successful. He had to make the difficult decision of whether to stay and watch over me or leave me alone in the house with my passed-out mother. Later, Cliff became a close family friend and my mother's AA sponsor.

One year later, my Mom recognized that her drinking had gotten out of control and sent me to live with my grandparents in Hampton, Virginia, for one year. During this time she voluntarily placed herself in a recovery facility called Turning Point for Women. I didn't mind the separation since I was thrilled to be spending time with Nana, Pa, and my uncles.

I especially liked being with my Uncle Rodney, who was only ten years my senior and more of a brother to me. He came across as a lovable teenager who was always getting himself into trouble.

After the year passed, my Nana accompanied me on my return to San Diego. My Mom's remarkable transformation to sobriety amazed me. My Nana called my Pa to let him know she and I had reached our destination, and they "had their Barbara back." My Mom had returned to my grandparents and me. She went back to school, enrolling at San Diego State where she studied Industrial Engineering. She landed a job in that field with a private company and began what would become her career until her retirement many years later.

At last, I had consistency and structure in my life. I went right back to attending school with the Leftons. I also started ballet classes, which became a passionate creative outlet for me.

***

Unfortunately, my Dad's football career ended prematurely due to back injuries. In 1966 he was traded from the San Diego Chargers to the Miami Dolphins, where he only played a few games. He had the option of undergoing spinal surgery—which risked paralysis—or retiring, and he chose the latter.

I suppose my Dad was fortunate that he was well educated and had interests outside of playing football. He loved coaching and mentoring young people, so it was a natural move for him to become a high school football coach as well as a history, gym, and driver's ed teacher. Later, he became a high school assistant principal and principal. He retired from the San Diego Unified School District as a school administrator.

It would be a major understatement to say that everyone admired and respected Earl Faison. His hulking size and booming voice commanded respect, but his slow moving gait and casual demeanor enabled people to feel at ease with him. When he entered a noisy room of students, you can be rest assured they silenced, sat up, and paid attention.

My Dad didn't entirely give up the limelight, however. While he pursued his career in education, he also found occasional work as a Hollywood television and film actor. Over the years he landed guest roles on episodes of several classic programs, including *The Beverly Hillbillies* (two episodes as "Earl Bell") and *The Six Million Dollar Man*. He played The Zombie in *Kolchak: The Night Stalker* and even had a line of dialogue in the Warren Beatty film *Heaven Can Wait.*

It shouldn't be surprising that my Dad brought me to a few Chargers games while I was growing up. He also took me along to see Indiana—his alma mater—in the Holiday Bowl in 1979 when I was around thirteen. Not only did the Hoosiers defeat the BYU Cougars 38-37 in a sensational game, my Dad introduced me to the president of Indiana who urged me to apply to the college (which I later did).

Although I cherished these moments with my father, I can't say that he was as present as I needed him to be. For most of my elementary school and teen years, I only saw him sporadically—maybe once or twice a year—and even on those occasions we didn't have opportunities to speak one-on-one. He attended occasional special events, such as my ballet performances; my debutante ball, sponsored by the Alpha Kappa Alpha Sorority; and my graduation. For the most part, however, he was only interested in my academic pursuits. He was self-absorbed to some extent and never found an appropriate way to connect with me in any kind of meaningful fashion, although we always said "I love you" to each other. Sadly, living separately for so many years, we never fully clicked as father and daughter. To this day, reflecting on my larger-than-life Dad, I am envious of the many students who were inspired and guided by him. I can't help but feel that I was cheated, and he invested in them more than me.

I guess it's kind of ironic that, despite my Dad's impressive professional football career as inspiration and my seemingly athletic build at five foot, eight inches, 126 pounds, I was far from being any kind of athlete. I couldn't dribble and run at the same time, so basketball was ruled out. I dabbled at other sports, such as volleyball and track but did not have natural talent at either, so I pursued other things, such as becoming a varsity cheerleader. Later, I donned a big red bird costume and served as "Cardinal," the school mascot.

Surprisingly, my father didn't seem to care one bit that I didn't play sports. Nor did he really pay much attention to my cheerleading, either. He was most attuned to my academic efforts and leadership skills and seemed genuinely impressed when I became senior class president.

***

I don't know whether not having my Dad around or having any kind of consistent father figure in my life impacted me. It's easy to speculate things like: Did this circumstance make me more vulnerable in some way to predators? Was I unprotected from male behavior—or naïve in some way?

Given the significant number of women and men of all ages who have been violated in some manner, I suspect that the things that happened to me over the years likely would have occurred anyway. On the other hand, having a six foot five, 270-pound all-pro football player Dad around me more often couldn't have hurt! Especially when it came to one emotionally painful situation—the first time I experienced abuse.

I always loved babies and gravitated to them. I was thrilled when Stacy—my cousin who also lived in San Diego with her husband, Todd—had a baby, and I could come over for visits. Either my Mom would take me or Todd would pick me up and drive me to their home. At first I enjoyed this because it gave me the opportunity to spend time with their infant and to swim and play tennis at their apartment building, which conveniently had a pool and tennis courts. Meanwhile, my time away afforded my Mom a much-needed break from single parenting.

Uncle Rodney gave my mother and me some stern warnings about my not going over to visit Stacy and Todd. Sometimes he spoke out so strongly against it that it led to screaming matches between him and my Mom. When I asked *why* I shouldn't go, his response was always something along the lines of "Stay away from them. I just don't trust them." But he left out the real reason he was so adamant. Likely, it was because back in those days people didn't even whisper a word about the awful subject—*molestation.*

My Mom had made it a habit of dismissing my uncle's concerns, probably because he was sixteen years her junior, and she didn't take him seriously. It didn't help that Uncle Rodney often acted like an immature teenager himself. But things were abundantly clear: He loved me deeply, wanted to protect me as best as he could, and knew there was something sinister about Todd.

Inevitably, I discovered the *why* behind Uncle Rodney's warnings. During one visit, after I had played tennis and gone for a swim, I returned to my cousins' apartment, where I lay down on the floor in my damp swimsuit and watched television. At some point, Todd sidled up next to me on the floor. I didn't think anything of it until his hand reached over to me, and he began exploring underneath my bathing suit.

I was completely unprepared for this: No one had ever given me any warnings about what to do if a man were to touch me in an inappropriate place. I didn't know how to react. I felt alarmed and frozen with fear.

Somehow I must have said *something* to express my displeasure and slipped over to the couch. When he joined me there, I retreated to the bathroom where I holed myself up and prayed to go home. Eventually I emerged and managed to get through the rest of day without being subjected to further advances.

I didn't tell anyone—not my Mom, Dad, or Uncle Rodney—about what happened, but after the incident I started to make up lame excuses about why I didn't want to go to see Todd and Stacy.

"I don't understand why you don't want to go there anymore," my mother would press me. "Don't you like swimming and playing tennis?"

I shrugged this off. There was no way I was prepared to admit what Todd had done to me.

I'm not sure whether my Mom was most interested in my interacting with family, being outdoors, or getting exercise—or if she just wanted more of her own "free time." Either way, she didn't give me any choice a couple of weeks later when she drove me back to Todd and Stacy's apartment building for another visit.

I reacted awkwardly around Todd and avoided eye contact with him. I did my best to steer clear of situations in which I would be alone with him, but this turned out to be impossible. It felt inevitable that *something* was going to happen and, sure enough, it did: He waved a pornographic magazine at me and tried to cajole me into looking at the lewd pictures with him. This time I was able to take a stronger stand. "Stop! Take that thing away," I protested. "I'm not looking at any of that with you..... Something is really wrong with you."

That was the extent of my second inappropriate encounter with Todd at his home. My mother continued to try to nudge me to go back for more visits, but I refused. She wasn't going to win. Not this time. Todd and Stacy kept calling and badgering both of us about my going over there, but I remained firm. After a while, they finally stopped asking, and Mom gave up trying to convince me. To say I felt relief would be a major understatement. I suspect my Mom was waiting for me to disclose my reasoning, but I never did and eventually she let it go.

Looking back, I wish Mom had paid closer attention to my apprehension and had heeded my uncle's warnings from the beginning. The experiences and emotions of having been violated stayed with me and taught me an invaluable lesson about not trusting people, especially around my children. I realized that anyone could be a child molester, and years later I protected my children like a grizzly. But little could I have known that this would not be the last time I would be forced into the role of victim myself.

***

I had a strong self-image as a teenager, despite the incidents of abuse and attending weekly AA meetings with my Mom. On the positive side of those meetings, I became close friends with Susan, whose mother was also an AA member. Together we passed the time having fun in the back of the room playing with our dolls.

Although I was blessed with beautiful skin, it always bothered me that I was not darker like my parents. I never wanted anyone to confuse me as either extreme—mixed race or white. I suppose everyone struggles with his or her identity to some extent while going through adolescence.

I was lucky to have had a good figure and, as mentioned, enough poise to make it as a varsity cheerleader and into the homecoming court. I worked hard at my studies and had plenty of friends and boys interested in me. My sense of self was strong, and I owe a great deal of my confidence to my Mom, who drilled into my head that there was nothing I couldn't do or become, and I believed her. Throughout my youth there was nothing my Mom wouldn't do or provide for me.

I admit that I wasn't immediately smitten by Chris. In fact, I'm not sure I even liked him much at first. There was something about him that gave me pause, but I couldn't put my finger on it.

Although he already had a girlfriend, Allison, he was relentless in his pursuit of me. He sent me flowers and came on strong. I remember saying to my friends that "He was too much, too quickly."

On the other hand, his tenacity was wearing me down. What young girl in her right mind *wouldn't* have been attracted to him? He was clean-cut with dark eyes and a light Chicano complexion. He had a muscular, athletic build and played varsity sports. He had a perfectionist streak, always dressing immaculately. As if that wasn't enough, there was something deeply seductive and charming about him. He could adapt to any environment and somehow find a way to make himself seem comfortable in even the most intimidating situations.

At first I was concerned that Chris's dad—a kind, hard-working blue collar guy—didn't care for me, probably because Allison was demure and sweet whereas I was opinionated, outspoken, independent, and headstrong. I think he saw that our future would be wrought with difficulties. But his opinion may have worked in my favor for us to get together. Teen boys always rebel against their parents, don't they?

Despite his dad's pleas to remain with Allison, Chris dumped her for me. I remember seeing Allison cry all over campus. While I felt bad for her and still had some apprehensions about Chris, I eventually caved in to his overtures and we became a couple.

Within a month we were head over heels in love and were hardly ever seen apart, attending every dance together arm-in-arm. We spent many romantic days and evenings at the beach. He constantly sent me flowers and other gifts. He taught me how to drive a manual transmission and didn't mind having me hang around with him and his baseball team pals. The sex was always good. He was a marvelous lover right from our initial intimate encounter, completely devoted to my satisfaction.

To outsiders, we probably seemed like the ideal couple—so much so that we were nominated as prom king and queen. We were destined for a fairytale life together, right?

Well, not exactly—far from it, in fact. We were both strong-minded, direct people who bickered all the time. He became irrationally suspicious of me and jealous of my ex-boyfriends, even though I remained faithful and had nothing whatsoever to do with them anymore.

Things became so heated between us that a major public blow up occurred in the high school quad the day before prom. I'm sure this is why we lost out on being voted prom king and queen to a far more deserving couple.

Despite all our highs and lows, the future looked bright for Chris and me in late spring 1983 as I set my sights on heading off to college. Since my childhood dream had been to become a surgeon, I planned to be pre-med and major in biology, so I could later attend medical school.

My Mom wanted me to attend Indiana University, where I would have had the "inside track" for admissions because my Dad was an alumni and had already planted some seeds for me to be accepted. I had two compelling reasons for wanting to remain closer to home and instead opted to attend the University of California San Diego (UCSD): my Mom was in remission from breast cancer, and I wanted to be near Chris, who was planning to take courses at a local community college in San Diego.

Admittedly, I struggled terribly at UCSD. I was a fish out of water in terms of being able to handle the workload. I worked tirelessly to keep up, but my pre-med friends and peers—who all went on to become successful doctors—were leagues ahead of me. Much later, I discovered that I have Attention Deficit Disorder (ADD). Who knows what I might have become if this had been known back then and I'd received the right treatment and tutoring.

It didn't help that Chris was a major distraction, often visiting me and staying over. I was drowning academically.

Someone from the school or my dorm called my Mom to inform her of how much Chris was sleeping over in my dorm room. Naturally, this led to a heated argument between Mom and me. "I'm not paying all of that money for Chris to be at the dorm with you," she warned. "You need to make a choice."

What can I say? I lied. I reassured her that Chris's presence was not in any way impacting my schoolwork and that I desperately wanted to succeed. I believed I could do both.

I ended up paying a severe price for not having heeded my mother's warnings. All my mistakes coalesced into something of a nightmare and destroyed my ambitions of ever going to medical school and becoming a doctor.

I became a pregnant teenager.

Chapter Two

FAMILY MEETING
San Diego, CA: January 1984-December 1984

My life had become a total train wreck. I went into the 1984 New Year as a broke, pregnant teenage college student.

I had little faith that Chris would want the baby, much less be any help to me raising him or her. Suffice it to say, Chris didn't have a college degree, any savings, or even a career path. Why would I expect him to bog himself down with a wife and child at such a young age without any prospects whatsoever? I steeled myself for his reactions as I showed up at his house with a onesie to convey the news. To my pleasant surprise, he was supportive of my decision to keep the baby and expressed genuine interest in being a father. This came as a major relief, although, I still had reservations about the two of us making it as a couple in the long run. Barely a week went by when we didn't have a major blow-up over some nonsense, but I was more than confident about my ability to be a loving mother with or without him.

Meanwhile, I kept my pregnancy secret from my mother for four and a half months. My rationale at the time was that I didn't want her to coerce me into doing anything rash, such as having an abortion. Although I believed in a woman's right to choose (and still do), I had already made my firm decision that I was going to have this child—no matter what. My mother could be dominating at times, occasionally to the point of throwing tantrums—or going off the rails completely—if she didn't get her way. Despite my age, I was confident that I could handle raising my baby, and I still clung to hopes of someday attending medical school. By intentionally holding out on informing my mother about my pregnancy for so many months, I was able to prevent her from meddling in my plans to be a mother.

It would be understating things to say she did not take the news well. She flipped out to such an extent that she drove herself to County Mental Health Hospital and asked to be committed. While she always struggled when it came to handling stressful situations, she did have a flair for the dramatic, and I should have anticipated she would find some way to become the central focus of my pregnancy. Fortunately, the staff at the mental hospital was able to take her off the cliff and get her through her emotional turmoil without admitting her or prescribing any drugs.

In retrospect, I suppose some of her reaction was understandable, given the circumstances. Chris and I were naïve kids and, by all accounts, helpless in terms of finding the means to support ourselves. My Mom had lived through eighteen years as a single parent and now fretted about my future, as well as the thought of having to raise the child all by herself. I never expected nor wanted anyone to raise the baby except for me.

Chris's parents, Mario and Rosa, weren't enthused by the news, either. Not that they were so perfect—far from it, in fact, as a couple and as parents. They constantly broke up—during which time Mario dated other women—and then got back together, only to split up again not long after that and restart the pattern.

I'm convinced that Rosa was the main issue in the relationship. I can't say whether she had any kind of specific emotional disorder, but it was clear to me that at the least she was dysfunctional. Throughout her marriage she would get in terrible moods and hide away in her bedroom for hours or even weeks on end without speaking to Mario (or anyone else, for that matter).

I was disturbed to learn what his mother had been like. She was manipulative and often used her son against his father. During arguments, Rosa would threaten to make a scene if Mario refused to talk to her. When Chris was a little boy, Rosa once held a knife to his throat to force his father to communicate with her during one of their spats. Mario always struck me as a decent, reserved kind of guy, and I felt sorry for the way Rosa treated him.

Chris's parents expressed their concerns about our having the child right off the bat. Chris firmly stood by my side, however, and did his best to counter their objections.

Then my Dad got involved: He called a "family meeting" with both sets of parents, Chris, and me. This was a big "uh oh" moment. One can only imagine how intimidated eighteen-year-old Chris felt having to face Earl Faison—a gigantic retired football pro—after having gotten his daughter pregnant.

The family meeting was tense from the start. Although snacks, *hors d'oeuvres*, coffee, and tea were served, no one touched any of it. An awkward silence filled the room for an unbearable amount of time, until…my Dad rose at the end of the table and spoke. (Later I discovered that he had told my Mom to restrain her comments, which she did…at least at first.) Although his voice was calm, my Dad's imposing stature and innate charisma took total charge of the room as he addressed Chris and me: "So. What's your plan?"

I could feel Rosa's eyes burning through me like she was somehow superior to me. I hardly even knew the woman at that time, but I felt judged by her—as if the situation was solely my fault.

After some hesitation, Chris summoned enough courage to fill the gap: "I will work full-time and support my family."

All at once both sets of parents chimed in. I don't recall who said what until, out of the blue, Rosa pointed at me and snapped: "*She is trying to trap him!*"

The gloves came off. My Mom, who had thus far kept reserved as promised, wasn't going to sit back for any of this. "Trap *what*? He has no education, no money—*nothing*! There's nothing to trap!" she fired back.

My Dad's cooler head prevailed as he gestured at Chris. "Here is what you are going to do: Sign up for the military. Enlisting in the service will bring in some income and at the same time provide security and medical coverage for your family. It will also offer a career path for you."

There was a slight pause as we processed his suggestion. Nobody could come up with a single objection or better plan. It was the only option that made any sense to the group, and my Dad had been the perfect person to deliver the message.

Chris agreed on the spot to enlist. Realistically speaking, even if it had been a bad idea, who was going to refuse Earl Faison?

***

Later that week, Chris was true to his word and headed to the Naval recruitment office, where he signed up to be a sailor and passed all the required medical tests. Luckily for us, San Diego had an established military community, and he was assigned to a boot camp at the local Naval Training Center starting in May.

Although Chris was following through on the plan, things remained tense between our two families. I was perplexed when my Mom demanded a private conversation with Chris before he headed off to boot camp. Something sounded off about this, so I pressed her for a reason. "I just want to talk to him, that's all," she answered.

I conceded, allowing the "private conversation" between them to occur. It didn't take long for things to turn ugly. My Mom requested that he formally apologize for having gotten me pregnant. He refused a couple of times and stormed out. Before he made it out the door, she attacked him from behind and scratched his back. To this day, I can't fathom how or why she behaved this way to him when he was at least trying to do right by her daughter.

Chris made it to boot camp without further incident, especially since I managed to keep him separated from my mother. Once he completed his training, he was conveniently assigned to a ship that was dry docked in San Diego. There was no indication his ship would ever head out to sea, which gave me comfort that Chris would remain close by in case I needed him.

The training seemed to go well for Chris, and I never heard him complain about it. He was always a neat, organized, and methodical type of guy, which is probably why he liked the Navy's regimental way of doing things. He demonstrated enough aptitude to become a skilled helicopter mechanic.

Meanwhile, I took time off from college after my second semester and moved back home with my Mom. I remember visiting Chris a few times at the base while very pregnant and seeing him either in his blue dungaree button down shirt and bell bottom pants or his pristinely pressed dress whites, which were the old-fashioned white sailor suit and hat.

On June 9, when I was in my ninth month, we decided to run off and get married, since neither of us wanted our child to be born out of wedlock. We went to a "dial-a-justice-of-the-peace" who performed wedding ceremonies at his home with his wife. We didn't invite anyone to the event that I remember, which was cut-and-dry and not the least bit romantic. But I felt safe and secure that I had a husband who was fully committed to helping support our child.

I missed Chris a lot and wrote to him several times. I imagined that, after the baby was born and Chris had completed his service, we would have an idyllic "Little House on the Prairie"-type of life. I probably should have been afraid of everything that lay in store for me—delivering a baby, raising him or her, and being married to a man I didn't get along with—but I wasn't. I was 100 percent certain that I could make it all work. I felt optimistic and perhaps even thrilled.

I also remained confident that I would return to college once the baby was born and settled. As I should have expected, my Mom had other ideas. She offered to take care of the baby—which was ironic, given her breakdown when she first heard the news of my pregnancy—if I were to transfer to Indiana, my Dad's proud alma mater and where his connections would have been beneficial to me. But I didn't want any part of a plan that involved separation from my baby. I required something for my child I never had for myself: a peaceful, coherent, two-parent family.

To help pass the time and have at least some access to education and the medical field, I took a phlebotomy course through a work-study program at the nearby Veterans Affairs hospital. I wasn't the least bit queasy drawing blood and became adept at finding the right spot for the needle insertion—especially when it came to learning to draw blood from men who had thick veins, which is easier. Interestingly, as unsanitary as it may sound, we didn't use gloves back then. (This later became a problem for me when gloves became required, as I couldn't get the right feel with them on.) My training also led to earning some extra money as a full-time phlebotomist. It goes without saying we needed every single penny to get ready for what lay ahead.

***

My due date came and went. Back in those days, doctors waited a lot longer than they do now to perform a C-section. Suddenly, I found myself three weeks overdue: The baby gave no signs of budging and just wouldn't drop. Realizing they had no choice, the doctors finally scheduled a C-section on July 9 at Sharp Hospital.

My obstetrician, Dr. Edward Kirshen, was a hippie who showed up in the delivery room wearing shorts, a colorful shirt that had a marijuana leaf on it and Birkenstock sandals. Chris was by my side as a screen was placed in front of my mid-section to separate our view from the doctor's work. I remained awake for the duration.

It became immediately apparent that things were not going well. My mellow hippie doctor spewed obscenities as he became increasingly frustrated while struggling to extract the baby. Apparently, my muscles were incredibly tight—perhaps from years of ballet—and just would not let go of the infant. Dr. Kirshen pulled, tugged, and wrenched…still nothing. His expletives worsened as time went on, and I admit Chris and I panicked. This just didn't seem normal or real.

At last, we heard the baby cry and Dr. Kirshen gleefully pronounced: "It's a girl!"

We named our child Ashley, after much debate over whether she should have that name or Vanessa. Although my head was in the clouds with her birth, things were far from easy for me in the beginning. I remained in the hospital for several days, which was common hospital practice back then. During that time Ashley didn't latch on to me right away to breastfeed, which made the nurses antsy and they tried to convince me to bottle-feed. I could feel them scowling at me as I struggled to make it work—which, eventually, I did.

I remember being in a great deal of pain while in the hospital and for several weeks thereafter. No doubt all of Dr. Kirshen's pulling and tugging was responsible for that. But I pushed my way through it and did the best I could to keep up with feedings and diaper changing. I did everything under the sun to be a good mother and read every parenting book or magazine I could get my hands on from cover to cover. I even found a "Mommy and Me" baby massage class for Ashley and me.

In terms of living arrangements, we were a bit fortunate in our timing. Mario had a fully furnished apartment that he had rented during one of his separations from Rosa. This was during one of the periods when they once again got back together, so Chris, Ashley, and I were able to move in and have some much-needed separation from our parents.

It was around this time that Ashley and I converted to Judaism. On the surface this probably sounds like it came out of left field—since I had few tangible connections to the religion—but it didn't. For my entire life I have been drawn to anything Jewish and had a firm belief in God. A friend once remarked that I have "a Jewish soul."

On my Mom's side of the family we had one relative, Sidney, who happened to be an Ethiopian Jew. I found both him and Judaism fascinating. In ninth grade, I inexplicably asked my Mom for a Star of David necklace. She bought it for me and didn't ask questions. I was the student who always questioned the explanations provided about faith. I was respectful and polite with my questions, yet never satisfied with the answers. We were taught to just believe in Jesus—which never made sense to me—and that was all we were expected to know.

Later, I met Terri Roseman—my senior class advisor in high school—who was Jewish. She didn't ever do anything to convince me to convert, but I was drawn to the prospect of having a Jewish family, and she was able to answer a lot of my questions about the religion. I read Lydia Kukoff's book, *Choosing Judaism,* and immediately knew that a Jewish life was exactly what I had been searching for.

On Terri's recommendation I spoke to a rabbi, visited a synagogue, and attended a Shabbos (Saturday) morning service for the first time. As I sat by myself in the back—a total stranger to this world—I was completely at peace and somehow felt right at home. I *belonged*.

Judaism allows and encourages questioning—even about God. This was a powerful statement to me. There were other tangible practices that made sense and held appeal, such as believing in one true God—not the Trinity, as Christians believe. I never agreed with the premise that only Christians could have access to heaven. Jews believe everyone can get in, as long as you live a righteous life. Jews don't proselytize; I loved that. Laws of *kashrut* seemed common sense. I like the fact that clergy are well educated teachers and don't claim to be closer to God than any other human being. I also appreciated the concept of keeping the Sabbath: the one day of the week designated to praying to God (and thanking him), meditating, and spending quiet time with family and friends without work. I wanted to convert to Orthodox Judaism and began the process with an Orthodox rabbi, as I didn't want there to be any question about my commitment to the religion. I also didn't want anyone to challenge Ashley's authenticity or mine.

Being Jewish was a completely natural calling for me. It was something I was always destined to do. I read everything I could about Judaism, took many classes, studied long and hard, and went to synagogue as often as I could. I fell in love with one thing in particular: blessing my child, Ashley, during Friday evening (Shabbos) observance at home. What a beautiful thing to do at the end of each week! During the blessing for girls, I followed my prayer book and, while placing my hand on her head, recited the following:

May you be like Sarah, Rebecca, Rachel, and Leah.

הָאֵלְוּ לְחַר הַקְבר הָרָשְׁכ סיהלֵא,הֵמיֹשִׁי.

May God bless you and guard you.

הָרְמֹשִׁיָוּ הָוֹהֵי,הֵכְרְבִי

May God show you favor and be gracious to you.

הֶנֶחִיוּ דָיְלָא וִיָנָּפ הָוהי רֵאִי
May God show you kindness and grant you peace.
סוּלְשׁ דָרְל מֶשִׂיו דָיְלָא וִיָנָּפ הָוהי אָשִׂי

The rabbi and all the congregants at the synagogue were always warm, friendly, and made me feel right at home. They didn't care the least about the color of my skin, so I never ever had to give that a second's thought or concern.

I dreaded explaining the conversion to my Mom and thought she was going to throw fits. But, unpredictable as always, she was delighted by the news. I thought my Mom might have been angry that she had struggled to send me to a small private Christian school for ten and a half years. As it turns out, during her early college years before her long-distance relationship with my Dad, she had been in love with a Jewish musician and wanted to convert to the religion back then.

I announced to my Dad I was converting to Judaism. He immediately said, "I assume that's because of your birth mom."

Puzzled, I asked: "What do you mean?"

He went on to explain that he and Mom were told my birth mother was Jewish and her last name was Bloom. After taking a few minutes to gather my thoughts, I explained to him that I would not have needed to convert if I had known this family history. (In Judaism, one is considered "Jewish" if the birth mother is Jewish.) Years later, I found out that there are Jewish relatives in my birth mother's family, but their history goes too far back in Europe to identify them. Maybe it was those relatives leading me back to my Jewish roots from many generations earlier. This yearning went unexplained until I converted.

Chris was a different story when it came to religion. He was born Catholic but didn't practice it at all. He didn't support my conversion and at first tried to talk me out of it. Eventually he realized he had no real say in the matter and dropped it. He personally never converted—I never forced the issue with him—and he drew the line at having a kosher household, which I wanted. (This did occur years later when we moved to Jacksonville.)

Religion barely skimmed the surface of our marital disagreements. Since Chris had an almost normal nine to five work schedule on base, he was around most mornings, evenings, and weekends unless he was assigned duty—time we spent endlessly bickering. We argued about pretty much anything and everything, but mostly one subject: money (since we didn't have any).

I tried my best to make a good home for us, but Chris was an obstinate perfectionist and hypercritical about my every move. He disliked my cooking and criticized how I kept the house and cleaned. Nothing was ever good enough for him and he barraged me with snide comments. He and his mother claimed that I "held Ashley too much" and was "spoiling" her. Rosa even went as far as saying that I was trying to "keep control" of the baby by nursing her. I didn't understand how it was possible to "spoil" a newborn or "control" her by breastfeeding, but I did my best to ignore both of them and carry on exactly as I was doing.

Chapter Three

LAURIE LANE
San Diego, CA: January 1985-August 1988

Although Chris was a caring and loving father, he was a terrible husband from day one. I was able to overlook certain things—or, maybe I just didn't know what the "norm" for newlyweds was. We weren't much more than children ourselves and neither of us was in any way prepared for marriage. Yes, we'd had a child together and shared the same name—but we could hardly be considered a "couple." Though we continued to have a certain physical attraction to each other, we had virtually nothing in common and experienced little in the way of genuine romance. We didn't know how to interact or communicate with each other and rarely went a full day without arguing over *something*.

It goes without saying we had poor examples of what healthy marriages looked like from our own respective upbringings. And, without a doubt, our individual personalities were too headstrong, which caused us to clash as a couple—especially when our financial situation came up.

I concede I wasn't the perfect wife for many of the same reasons Chris had been a subpar husband. I was intensely focused on raising Ashley and, in retrospect, was unable to be as attentive to him as he would have liked.

As I was gradually beginning to recognize, there was something baleful lurking behind Chris's good looks, charm, and polish. His controlling and dominating nature barely hinted at the darkness that resided underneath. The friction between us increased because I refused to put up with his erratic behavior and frequently stood up to him.

His dark side began to emerge in the form of suspicious and paranoid behavior. I should have been concerned when I noticed that he was following me around the house and spying on me when I least expected it. He eavesdropped on my phone conversations, intent on finding out what I was saying about him.

One evening I was on a phone call with my friend Terri. It was early evening and I thought Chris would be gone for hours, since he had told me he would be working late for duty. I always preferred connecting with people while he was out of the house, as I could feel more comfortable and speak freely. Even so, just to be safe, I stretched the antenna out of our cordless phone as far as it would go and stepped outside to the right of our building to be doubly sure I had ample privacy.

"Terri," I confided. "I'm really worried about how things are going with Chris. He's always been controlling and hypercritical about me—but lately he seems to be on edge.... The other day he said I talk to my friends too often."

Terri had an open ear and was always supportive when I vented to her. She also tried her best to help reduce some of my irritation and keep my family drama down to a minimum. She was a good sounding board for me and offered helpful advice. "You know marriage is so hard even under the best circumstances. Have the two of you considered marital counseling?"

I'm not sure exactly what I said in response, but it was probably along the lines of "counseling is a good idea" even though at that point I didn't know how Chris would react to it. I revealed to her that I was fed up with our constant arguments over nonsense. I had a hard time dealing with his barrage of criticism, especially since I was working at night in the hospital lab trying to nap at the same time as Ashley in order to avoid childcare costs and to be with her as much as I possibly could.

Inexplicably, my heart froze: I felt a stinging presence looming around the corner. Suddenly, appearing as if from nowhere, Chris snatched the phone from me and hurled it a far distance away. I heard it smash against the ground.

My mind raced to what I might have said that he had overheard. I screamed: "What is wrong with you! What are you doing!"

He stormed off as if to say, *I can't hear what you are saying, so you're not saying it.*

I didn't bother to look for the phone; I knew it was broken and useless. I headed upstairs and grabbed Ashley. "I'm going to my Mom's," I informed him.

He didn't seem to care at all and we left.

Meanwhile, Chris confided in his dad about our marital issues. I didn't understand why he thought it was all right for him to seek counsel from others, but apparently I wasn't entitled to do the same.

I ended up speaking with his parents about our struggles. *Why not?* I figured, since our dirty laundry was out in the open anyway. Maybe, I thought, they would have some insights into Chris and offer helpful advice.

According to Mario, the stress of paying the rent was too much for Chris and explained why he was always on edge. That made some sense to me; if only he could have expressed it to me directly. It seems that we heard and understood each other a lot better when we were separated and through a third party. Still, being aware of this wasn't nearly enough for me to forgive or forget Chris's explosive behavior.

Gradually, Chris managed to chip away at my resolve. He made repeat visits to my Mom's house to convince me to return home. He swore he would act more pleasant around me and not be as demanding. He even said he was open to considering marital counseling. Most of all, he stressed the importance of a father being around for our daughter's benefit.

"Don't you want an intact family for Ashley?" he would repeat to me while turning up the charm.

Yes, I very much wanted this. I always wanted my daughter to have a father present. I wanted her to have what I saw on *Little House on the Prairie*: Charles Ingalls. I knew it was an unrealistic fairytale, but at the same time I couldn't accept her growing up with an absent father, as I did.

The clincher for overlooking his behavior and allowing him to move into my Mom's house was that the lease on Mario's apartment was expiring. There was no way Chris and I could afford the place, and Mario certainly couldn't pay for it on his own. After weeks of deliberation, we decided it might be best for him to join us. Although Chris and Mom didn't get along, we didn't think we had any other choice due to our financial situation. My Mom only asked for a minimal contribution from us, mainly the utilities, which eased our minds about bills, debt, and paying for Ashley's necessities.

Things were strained right from the beginning. If Chris and I were like oil and water, he and my Mom were like gasoline and a match. The three of us together were at a Chernobyl level of explosiveness.

Seemingly little things became huge blow-ups between Mom and Chris. Every week both sought to be the first to tackle the Sunday newspaper—especially the Sports section—and find it in pristine condition, untouched by human hands except for the newspaper boy. When either managed to snatch the newspaper off the porch, the other person would complain to me about it and drag me in the middle. I always had to side with my Mom. After all, we were just guests in her house—and not fully paying ones, at that.

Around this time, my Mom became very close with Ashley, who followed her around the house and looked like "her little shadow." Predictably, Chris found fault with Mom's grand-parenting style, considering her to be too lenient when Ashley misbehaved or was uncooperative, which wasn't an excessive amount for a toddler. Mom tended to dote on her grandchild and let the small stuff go, as most grandparents would. Chris was of the old school "spanking" mentality, whereas I preferred timeouts—with rare spankings for extreme situations only—and found this to be a more effective way to enforce discipline. Chris believed timeouts to be a "total waste of time," as it were.

Even food choices became a source of contention. I wanted my daughter to eat healthy, nutritious foods. I wasn't trying to go overboard by becoming rigidly organic, I just wanted Ashley to avoid the crap. Chris, on the other hand, grew up with a different cultural perspective and saw nothing wrong with fried foods and fatty meats, such as pork, which were staples in his family's upbringing. He loved sugary drinks like Kool-Aid and regularly offered them to our daughter. "If it was fine for me to drink it, it's fine for her," he said.

Chris didn't approve of anything I did—parenting or otherwise. He was opposed to my attending La Leche League International meetings. He disliked my sending Ashley to pre-school at the Jewish Community Center, which I regarded as essential for her social development and religious education. He complained about my attending synagogue on Friday nights and Saturday mornings. And he discouraged me from taking adult education classes during my spare time between phlebotomy hours and caring for Ashley. I still held out hope of someday returning to school full-time, getting my undergraduate degree, and maybe even attending medical school, though these ambitions were growing dimmer with each passing day.

Perhaps most of all, he objected to my protectiveness when it came to Ashley. As a result of my childhood experiences with Todd, I was suspicious of pretty much anyone being alone with her. I made it clear to my Mom that she keep her eyes on Ashley at all times when she was under her care and never leave her with anyone—not even for a minute. She understood my directions and had no problem with it.

I trusted Chris's parents, as well as his sister, with Ashley in situations where it was just the three or four of them, but when it came to gatherings and public situations, I felt diligence was still needed, even with extended family. Chris thought I was extreme with my demands and did not see any risk or threat whatsoever.

I was well aware that things were way off between Chris and me; we were light years apart and knew exactly which buttons to press to upset each other. I felt somewhat assured that he seemed amenable to our going to marital counseling. The concept didn't noticeably cast any stigma in his mind, since his parents had been back and forth with marital counseling for years. Unfortunately, each time I brought up setting up an appointment he put it off by saying, "I promise, I'll be better to you. I won't nitpick so much... and I'll control myself from snapping again." At one point he had the gall to say to me, "If you would just be quiet and not say anything, everything would be fine."

Well, I was not one to remain silent. Never. Not for anyone.

Finally, after all the delays and excuses, we went to marital counseling. The sessions helped somewhat—especially in terms of communication—but the positive results were only temporary. After a while, the same behaviors resurfaced, and we aggravated each other all over again, so the counseling visits gradually dwindled until they came to an end altogether.

Although Chris and my Mom's relationship progressively improved over time, they certainly were not best buds. My relationship with his parents also improved and they softened up with me. I trusted them enough to solicit their advice in dealing with Chris and, frankly, improve his behavior toward me. They made some effort—probably out of love for Ashley, as they would have done anything to help keep the peace for her benefit—and had some successes here and there. However, there was only so much they could control about his nature.

After two and a half years of Mom, Chris, Ashley, and me residing under the same roof, a radical change occurred. Mom was transferred to another site with her job at General Dynamics, which meant she had to relocate to Long Beach.

This had both a positive and negative impact. On the plus side, Ashley was separated from her Nana, with whom she had developed such a close bond. It also greatly reduced the tension in the house because Chris had one less person to argue with and no one with whom to joust over the Sunday newspaper.

All of this was negated by our worsened financial predicament. Although we had the house all to ourselves and the additional room and freedom that went with it, we now had to cope with paying my Mom rent, so she could cover the mortgage and all the home care costs ourselves. This was only fair to my Mom, of course, but Chris and I had barely made ends meet when we just covered utilities. Chris's military salary and my earnings from being a phlebotomist never seemed to cut it, so the additional financial burdens took their toll on our already taxed relationship.

***

It was something of a silent blessing for me when we found out that Chris was being shipped out to sea for a test run on his ship after years of having been dry-docked in San Diego. His hiatus, albeit brief, would give me a much-needed break from all our disputes and finally offer a quiet, peaceful home for Ashley.

The few months while Chris was away were highly liberating for me, to say the least. At long last I could do what I needed to do without being hammered by his constant disparagement. I was able to expand and deepen my friendships and speak on the phone with them without worrying about whether Chris was hiding around the bend listening in, ready to break another phone.

I must admit: It was one of the happiest times of my life. I actually *enjoyed* myself. I loved being a mother. Ashley and I did everything we could together. San Diego's temperate climate meant we could go out and about any day we wanted when I wasn't at work and she wasn't in preschool. We were outside pretty much all the time. This gave Ashley the opportunity to socialize in playgroups, frolic on the beach, and roam bookstore and library aisles. We rode our bikes and strolled around shops in quaint Seaport Village. Best of all, our annual membership at the magnificent San Diego Zoo enabled us to spend entire weekends there.

I also found an easy way to make a little extra money by selling Discovery Toys at home parties. While my compensation wasn't much, the benefit of being able to own these high-quality, educational products—i.e., stacking toys—and have Ashley play with them for free was a wonderful perk.

I won't mischaracterize things and say we didn't miss Chris. We did. It was more difficult to get things done around the house without him, and certainly Ashley missed her father, who had always been good to her. He contributed his share around the house and involved himself in Ashley's activities with sincere interest. There are always adjustments military families must make when a member goes off on a tour of duty. I felt guilty about having so much fun without him—but, admittedly, not *super* guilty. Ashley and I spent plenty of time visiting Chris's parents and sister to keep his side of the family involved.

As it happens, Chris was born for the military lifestyle and performed well as a sailor. He was always immaculate in his presentation and thrived on having a set of strict rules at all times. He liked to toe the line when it came to performing his duty. He moved up the ranks pretty quickly, earning promotion after promotion.

Then, one day, he returned home from his tour in Asia. Despite everything that had happened between us, I was happy to see him and have him home. Ashley, who was gifted with a cute stuffed panda bear from Japan, was delighted to have her dad back. I was optimistic that being overseas and away from us had given him some time to reflect about things and change his attitude toward me. I won't go as far as saying we were the Ingalls, but for that brief period we were able to have a fresh start and find a glimmer of hope and happiness together.

As fate would have it, we were next thrown yet another curveball.

Chapter Four

PRIORITIES
San Diego, CA: September 1988-April 1991

In the months while Chris was away, I had made certain to go on the birth control pill to be prepared for his return home. Between our rocky marriage and always-tight financial situation, I did not want to take any chances and complicate our lives by getting pregnant again.

Prior to going on birth control, I always knew when I was ovulating because I experienced the same pain every twenty-eight days like clockwork. When I continued to feel the discomfort of ovulation while on the pill, I called my OB/GYN to find what was going on. The doctor assured me it would not repeat the following month and urged me to continue taking the pill every day. When it happened again four weeks later, I called him a second time. His response? "Carry on as you've been doing. This is normal."

The ovulation symptoms occurred the third consecutive month. By this time, Chris had returned home from overseas duty, and we became intimate right away. How could we not after having been apart for so many months?

Weeks later, we confirmed I was pregnant. I learned the hard way that the pill is not an infallible method of birth control. Or, maybe it's that some women on it *are* fallible in terms of not taking it consistently, which messes with its effectiveness. Either my irregular times were at fault or I had a lapse in memory and forgot to swallow it one day. It's also entirely possible that my then-undiagnosed ADD was at fault. Who knows?

Whatever the reason—ineffectiveness or carelessness—I was faced with my second unplanned pregnancy at only twenty-one years of age. Once again I was unwilling to have an abortion. I strongly felt that my children should have the same father; at least I could provide them with that. In fact, although Chris and I were hardly prepared as a couple to have another child, I was more than fine with the situation and committed to raising him or her with the same love and affection as Ashley.

At first Chris felt otherwise and wanted me to have an abortion. Ultimately, he realized there was simply no persuading me and gave in. Over time, he came around to adjusting to the idea of being a father again. But he continued right where he left off with his poor attitude and nasty behavior toward me, once again being judgmental about the same-old things: managing money; cooking and housekeeping; and child-rearing issues, such as discipline and nutrition. He almost always tried to derail any plans I made with my friends that didn't involve him. Chris's time away hadn't changed him the slightest bit.

I have no doubt that our marital stress caused our child to be premature by a dangerous amount of time—eleven weeks. On September 8, 1988, Ashley and I attended her preschool orientation at the Jewish Community Center (JCC), after which we planned to watch Chris play softball. On our way out we stopped at the bathroom. I completed my business, left the stall, and went to the sink to wash my hands. Before I had a chance to turn on the faucet my water broke. I had no idea what to make of my situation or how to react properly because I hadn't gone through this with Ashley's birth.

I calmly stepped out into the hallway with Ashley, heading straight toward the red pay phone booth even though Terri was seconds away from me at the orientation.

I can't explain my thinking at the time, except to say that I didn't want to alarm her—or Ashley. I dumped some coins in the slot and dialed my doctor's emergency number. The answering service was able to get hold of the on-call OB/GYN right away. He called me, from all places, a pay phone at a San Diego Padres game. He screamed over the noise of the crowd: "Just answer my questions: How far are you? Did you say your water broke?"

I responded to him as loud and clear as I could. He told me to rush straight to the hospital. I hung up, inserted more coins, and dialed Rosa, who snapped into action. I drove home with Ashley, where we were met by Chris's mom—who took me to the hospital—and Chris's sister, who remained to babysit.

We didn't say a word to each other during the drive. My mind focused on the worst possible scenarios, and I knew Rosa was worried sick. I was terrified, too, at what might transpire while delivering a 29-week-old baby.

Meanwhile, Mario carried the news to the ball field, where Chris was in the middle of his softball game. When Mario summoned him to be by my side at the hospital during my medical emergency, Chris had the nerve to ask for more time to finish playing the game. Clearly, my husband was ignorant when it came to understanding the gravity of heading into childbirth at only twenty-nine weeks. His father had to prod him into leaving, which he finally did.

I was taken to Scripps Hospital in La Jolla, where I had been working as a phlebotomist. The doctor on call—the same one who had left the Padres game mid-inning for my emergency—stood at reception, anxiously waiting for me. He did not look happy. I'm pretty sure he was wondering what had taken me so long to get there when he had given me express verbal orders to shoot directly to the hospital.

The medical team scrambled to care for me, placing me in a private room with my own bathroom. "I don't want the baby to be born now," I protested along the way. "It's too early. I don't want my child to have any challenges…"

"It's not up to you," one of the nurses declared. "We'll do the best we can."

It actually helped that she was so frank. There were no decisions to be made. Everything was beyond my control.

The staff tested me for all kinds of things, such as Group B strep, to determine what might have caused my water to break. They performed an amniocentesis to see if the baby was suffering from any abnormalities and how developed the baby's lungs were. So far, everything checked out okay. The doctors placed me on steroids intravenously for eighteen hours to develop the baby's lungs as much as possible while staving off delivery. Meanwhile, at some point Chris and his father made it to the hospital, as did my Mom coming in from Long Beach.

I lay in the hospital for some time hooked up to monitors that didn't show any sign of contractions or anything else out of the ordinary. The nurses forbid me from moving around but lying there for so long made me fidgety.

As it happened, earlier in the day—not having had the slightest inkling that this would be the delivery date—I'd eaten a substantial vegetable lasagna for lunch. Well, that delightful meal came back to haunt me as I threw up the entire colorful feast into a hospital bucket. As if that wasn't enough, my lower back started to hurt—*a lot.*

Restless and in excruciating pain, I had a lapse in judgment and tried standing up—even though I was attached to a catheter and all kinds of other equipment.

My Mom, who always had a flair for the dramatic, swung open the door of my room and hollered into the hallway toward the nursing station: "She's getting up! She's getting up!"

The nurses swooped in and cajoled me onto my back in the nick of time.

Little did I know that if I had risen to my feet there was a high probability of the baby dropping right out of my uterus, smashing to the floor, and dying.

It took far too long for the nursing team to deduce that I was already in labor. Although nothing was showing up on the monitor, vomiting and extreme back pain are two signs that something was progressing towards dilation.

After a few minutes, the on-call doctor who had met me and started the steroids was still on duty and scurried in to check up on me. He signaled it was time. A herd of nurses stampeded the room to wheel me into the hallway.

"Did someone call Children's Hospital?" I asked anyone who would listen.

I was well aware that Scripps did not have a neonatal intensive care unit (known as a NICU), which would be essential in the care of any premature newborn. I grew panicked that my soon-to-be-born child would be in a facility that was ill prepared to handle whatever complications lay in store for him or her.

Unwilling to be ignored, I repeated my question but in a much testier tone of voice: *"Did someone call Children's Hospital?"*

One of the nurses finally replied, "There's no time."

At least I had my answer. I would have to deal with that issue later. Right then I needed to focus on my current situation: delivering this baby.

It didn't take long once I was set up in the delivery room. Chris joined me in there wearing a yellow gown, but we said nothing to each other. The baby was arriving so early neither of us had any time to prepare. He seemed numb and scared while trying his best to stay out of everyone's way.

I pushed once, maybe twice, and my fragile little baby came out without uttering a peep. No crying whatsoever; I doubt the poor thing had the strength. I couldn't get much of a look at my baby from my angle; all I could discern was a head full of hair. I lay powerless to assist my sweet little one.

Before I had a chance to gaze further, the baby was whisked away and bagged for oxygen. It had all happened with such frenzy that no one bothered to take notice of the gender.

Doctors and nurses huddled in a corner around the baby. I heard one of them indicate the baby was successfully taking in oxygen, which I interpreted as a good sign. I became aware of the OB/GYN sitting at the edge of my bed, essentially twiddling his thumbs.

"Can someone please tell me if I had a boy or girl?" I blurted.

Apparently, the doctor himself didn't know, since he was preoccupied with the grave circumstances of the delivery. He rose from the bed to join the others who were crowded around the baby and peeked in at his first window of opportunity. A few expectant moments later he returned to his spot next to me on the bed and announced, "It's a girl."

I processed the news.

A girl. A teeny-tiny, helpless little girl.

I prayed that she would be okay.

Everything will turn out all right.

The doctor resumed twiddling his thumbs.

"If you don't mind, doctor," I interrupted his important business. "Are you waiting for something?"

"Why yes," he answered. "I'm waiting for the placenta to come out."

"Oh."

When this failed to happen by itself, he decided to take the bull by the horns, as it were. He attempted to manually tug on the umbilical cord, which was still attached to the placenta; unfortunately, it broke apart, and he had to do a procedure known as dilation and curettage—D&C, for short—to clean the tissue out of my uterus. Suffice it to say, this was not a pleasant experience.

As I eventually discovered, Alese—the name Chris and I bestowed upon her—was born three pounds, one ounce, which is actually larger than usual for a 29-week-old preemie.

The doctor informed me that the steroids were what had enabled her to survive. Still, she was a far cry from being out of the woods. My coworkers in the lab—who were unrestricted by HIPPA laws back then—watched her stats drop and become increasingly critical.

***

Every day is a new adventure when you have a preemie, and I imagined and fretted about all kinds of worst-case scenarios. You never know what can go wrong. I sat with her every day and stared at her through the incubator glass, caressing her constantly, yet unable to hold or nurse her. I had begun pumping breast milk, which they fed to her through a small tube. The machinery sounds were constant reminders of her fragile condition. I watched her monitors like a hawk, as if I was an authority on interpreting medical readings.

Three days passed after the delivery. I had recovered by this point, and they wanted to discharge me from the hospital. But how could I leave my helpless baby all alone when so many bad things might happen? I tried every argument imaginable, but the staff said they had no choice and discharged me as a patient. Their hands were tied, as my insurance would not cover my staying any longer.

I became hysterical while standing by Alese's side. I continued sobbing as I sat in the lobby waiting for Chris to pick me up. The trauma of being separated from her was too much for me to bear. I was emotionally ripped apart. To make matters worse, Chris was a no-show. I couldn't understand where he was and what he was doing. The nurses did their best to comfort me as I waited...and waited...and waited...until Chris finally appeared in his softball jersey. His team had been competing in a tournament, and he didn't feel he could miss it. Priorities!

Alese spent only a week at Scripps Hospital. We worked with a pediatrician who specialized in neonates, but plainly the facility was not equipped to handle preemies. We became frustrated because Children's Hospital didn't have room to care for her and had no choice except to refuse her. We were then told that the Navy had a superb NICU as part of its hospital. Chris's Navy service paid off for us in this instance, as Alese was admitted without any hassle.

The medical ambulance rushed Alese to the Navy NICU. Chris and I sped over to join her there, but, in our haste to enter the hospital and see her, we left my breast milk in a cooler in the back seat of the car. I felt foolish about our terrible oversight because we knew it would be spoiled by the time we would be able to retrieve it. This became another source of irritation. Colostrum in a mother's breast milk is extra vital in helping boost the development and immunity for preemies. Our baby needed every fighting advantage she could get.

On arrival we were told the devastating news that the baby would likely need to remain in the NICU for *nine to eleven weeks*. This seemed like an eternity. We hadn't even held her yet, and I certainly wasn't permitted to breastfeed her directly. How I longed to bring her home and place her safely in her bassinet.

We did our best to adjust. The Navy had a highly skilled nursing staff and a brilliant neonatologist, so we felt more secure with the new care. I was at the hospital every single day at all hours; sometimes I went home to sleep, but more often than not I remained by her side. Chris joined me right after work. We would stare at the monitors for hours. After a few days they allowed us to finally hold her in our arms, which we did whenever we were told it was safe to do so.

The irony is that I don't think Chris and I were ever closer as a couple than during this intense time. We were so consumed with our baby's health that we didn't have a chance to argue. His softball game lapses aside, Chris seemed genuinely concerned and upset with our daughter's welfare and eased up on his perfectionism about everything large and small. Chris's parents and sister took good care of Ashley when she wasn't in preschool, so we could be with Alese at the hospital.

We both had a major scare when we were told that Alese's red cell count wasn't strong enough, and she needed a blood transfusion. This was at the height of the AIDS crisis, a time when the medical community didn't have enough of a handle on ensuring safe blood donations. I wasn't going to take any chances and pressed the resident for answers: "Who are the donors? Has the blood been fully tested?"

The resident was stunned by my blunt questions. I was a fireball when it came to patient advocacy and apparently no one had ever dared challenge her before. Somehow she alleviated my concerns enough for me to allow the transfusion procedure to take place. The resident also informed me that the NICU had a small group of designated donors, which put my mind at ease. Since Alese was so little, the blood could only be introduced in small quantities at a time. Gradually, the process took effect and her red blood cells improved.

I trusted the nurses and doctors at the NICU and knew they were the cream of the crop—but that didn't stop me from going overboard with questions and demands. I didn't care what they thought. Having worked in a hospital I knew all too well the things that could potentially go awry. I wasn't going to take any chances when it came to my baby's health. My scrutiny of the staff and relentlessness gave me something of a reputation around the NICU as an over-protective mother hen, but I didn't care.

After having spent so much time at the hospital engrossed in my daughter's incubator, I began to pick up vibes about the nurses and did some backseat supervising. Most of them were sharp as a tack and went about their business with professional ease and finesse. When they were low on staff, however, I caught a less experienced nurse struggling to change the arterial line connecting to Alese's artery in the center of her body. The nurse seemed perplexed as her mind reviewed through the steps: *step one, step two, step three.* I was not at all confident she knew what she was doing and asked for the nurse manager. I demanded that a new nurse be assigned to change the arterial line. The nurse manager complied and replaced the bumbling nurse with someone more capable who finished the job without any problem.

Later that day, I caught a glimpse of Alese's chart. The nurse manager had scrawled a few words on it in all red letters, uppercase, and with exclamation marks: "VERY DIFFICULT MOTHER!!!" Again, I didn't care. In fact, I thought it was kind of amusing and flattering. I wasn't ever going to allow a mistake to happen to my child.

Not long after that, Alese needed a spinal tap. Nothing can prepare a parent for the emotional devastation of witnessing this being inflicted upon her baby. Alese scrunched her face in agony as they poked and squeezed at her back. She tried to cry, but she was still too weak and couldn't produce a sound. I was horrified to the point of readying myself to harm someone. Somehow Alese—and I—managed to get through it.

We had an even more dramatic event while Alese remained in intensive care. Shortly after a baby is born, a valve in the heart automatically closes. This often fails to occur for preemies, and Alese was no exception. The open valve prevented her from fully taking in the needed amount of oxygen.

We met with the lead neonatologist, who explained the corrective procedure to Chris and me. Alese would have had a surgical line directed from her belly all the way across her back. They told us it was essential and urged us to sign off on it. We told them we would give it some thought.

After much deliberation, Chris and I mutually agreed to decline the surgery. It seemed way too radical to perform on this child after all she'd been through. It also seemed like it might cause long-term scarring and perhaps other residual complications. The neonatologist reacted insulted and shocked. Who were we to say "No" to him? What did we know? He was the all-important surgeon, while we were just ignorant kids.

Fortunately, there was an alternative: a series of three doses of drugs aimed at closing the valve. Every day the technicians checked the ultrasound; every day the valve had failed to close.

Once again the doctors implored us to approve the surgery. They tried assuring us that she would be fine afterward. She'd grow and the scars would heal. But Chris and I stuck to our guns and refused.

The doctors grudgingly put Alese on a fourth trial of meds. Two weeks later, the valve still hadn't closed. Now we didn't have a choice: We were putting her life at risk by not agreeing to the surgery. Chris and I talked it over and caved in.

The dreaded day of the surgery came. Our parents had all arrived at the hospital to wait with us. Standard procedure requires that the technician perform one last ultrasound beforehand. Miraculously, it had closed on its own that very morning and Alese no longer needed the surgery.

To this day, I have no idea why Chris and I had so much faith in our decision to put it off. However it happened, it proved to be the right call, and we didn't need to speak with the neonatologist again after that.

***

Alese spent a total of four weeks at the Navy NICU. Once she was in the clear, it was safe to transfer her back to Scripps.

At long last, we were given permission to hold her regularly. Words could not describe our joy. We had all been through so much, and now it looked like all our prayers and devotion had paid off.

I continued to spend every possible moment at the hospital with her. One of the doctors—someone I worked with—had the nerve to chide me for spending so much time at her side. "What is the matter with you? You never go home. You won't leave your child. What about your other child? Aren't you being neglectful to her?"

He upset me so much with the unprovoked attack that the other nurses came around to console me.

How dare he accuse me like that!

Maybe he thought he was entitled to say this because we'd worked alongside each other, and he was sincerely attempting to give me helpful advice, even though it came off as condescending and judgmental. I don't know. Either way, I believed he was way out of line.

The truth was, although I trusted and respected the doctors and nurses, I viewed them as mere human beings capable of making mistakes. I didn't want to be the one to suffer any kind of loss because someone was having a bad day and missed something or had a rare lapse in judgment. I learned that, when it comes to medical care, you must pay attention, you have to question, and you have to be an assertive advocate.

***

Six weeks later—a lot sooner than we originally expected—the hospital part of our ordeal was over. Chris and I went home with a beautiful baby girl. We couldn't have been more thrilled.

We were provided with special care instructions, some of which mattered and some did not. Regarding the latter, I was told not to nurse the baby directly because it required too much effort for a preemie, and she would lose too much weight. For the first couple of days we fed her breast milk from a bottle with a bigger hole. I thought this was silly and ignored the recommendation on the third day. She took to breastfeeding just fine and made excellent progress gaining weight.

Visitors—such as my Dad and his second wife—were welcome in our house, but they had to wear masks and gloves when in the room with her, as she was still susceptible to germs. Even with such precautions and all the frequent checkups, hearing tests, and developmental assessments, she still contracted frequent colds and infections because of her weakened immune system. I recalled the earlier blood transfusion she had undergone and insisted on an AIDS test; thankfully, the results were negative.

Alese was placed on a small dose of prophylactic antibiotics. This changed her whole life: The illnesses stopped, and her body found a rhythm. We were able to plan for her baby naming. We invited a few friends, family, and my rabbi for the small ceremony at my home. Aside for some allergies and some knee issues that surfaced over the years, Alese led a stable, healthy life subsequent to her first two years.

Terri, who had spent her career in teaching and in special education, sat me down early on to prepare me to look out for signs of common occurrences among preemies, especially learning disabilities. I didn't take any offense, deferring to her expertise and taking it all in: better to be safe than sorry. Fortunately, none of these possibilities ever became a real concern.

Eventually, Alese was given the green light to be taken outside in the stroller. I preferred to keep her close to my body when we were out in public, so I carried her in the front baby carrier attached to my chest. She was so small that passersby couldn't see any of her and presumed the carrier was empty.

Everything seemed to be falling into place, and we worked toward establishing some semblance of normalcy and routine as a family. Mom went back to Long Beach and was then relocated to work in Texas. Ashley and Alese bonded as sisters. I returned to work part-time as a phlebotomist at the hospital. Chris continued to serve locally in the Navy.

But a "normal relationship" was never remotely possible between Chris and me. Our truce ended shortly after Alese entered our home. Once again Chris reverted to his hypercritical habits and tried to control me. We quarreled about major and minor issues with equal hostility.

I knew something drastic had to be done to shake things up other than separating my girls from their father, and believed I found the perfect solution.

Chapter Five

SHOJI ROOM
Atsugi, Japan: May 1991-April 1994

The Navy offered service people in good standing like Chris an interesting relocation opportunity: They and their families had the option of switching where they were stationed—to Florida or somewhere more economical. However, for a family like mine to qualify, there was one obligatory rite of passage: We had to first live overseas. We could choose whichever military base we wanted, as long as there was an open spot for Chris's specific job.

A move overseas struck me as highly appealing. I felt I had to go somewhere new—far away from San Diego. Our marriage wasn't stable, and I could no longer hide behind the excuse that we were "young." Chris and I were truly struggling. The bonding we experienced getting through the trauma of Alese's premature birth failed to strengthen our relationship. While we both loved our two beautiful children, being parents together only increased the amount of friction and range of topics for us to argue about.

To this day, I continue to question my judgment staying with Chris for so long, given the extent of our incompatibility. When it comes down to it, I continued to cling to the possibility of our *Little House on the Prairie* life coming true, even though it was just a pipe dream. Each time I came close to deciding to split from Chris, I imagined my daughters being raised by a single parent without their father, and God knows what kind of step-parenting situation the girls might have been subjected to. I remembered how much I missed my own father growing up, and how my Mom had struggled to do everything on her own.

Then there was our never-ending money issue. We could barely afford to live in my mother's house. How could Chris sustain a separate place to live while contributing to support the rest of us? I also had my doubts that Chris could be trusted to pay alimony and child support, especially if he felt I had hurt him by splitting us up.

A change of pace abroad sounded like an exciting way for us to get a fresh start in completely new surroundings. While I cared for Chris's family and appreciated their occasional help, I also believed some separation from them underfoot would be beneficial to us.

With all of this in mind, I asked Chris to put in for an overseas request. He didn't balk at the decision. It didn't take long for him to be approved and receive a three-year assignment in Atsugi, Japan, with us in tow. It was a major move for our family, and we had no idea what to expect or how to prepare. My young girls were distraught over leaving their friends, grandparents, and house—which we arranged for renters on behalf of my Mom during our absence—but they handled it well considering their ages (now three and seven) and we went into it together like it was a great big adventure.

One major benefit of being relocated by the military is that they really know how to pack and ship stuff. We didn't have to do much of anything and trusted that our possessions were in safe hands as the men prepared the boxes to be transported by boat. Mostly everything went to Japan, except for my piano and a few other things, which were placed in storage.

We vacated our house and headed to LAX Airport. The excitement turned anti-climactic when our takeoff was delayed several hours. I remember Chris and me sitting by the gate—a child asleep on each of our laps—with a long row of our suitcases in front of us.

Eventually, we took off to embark on our great big adventure and arrived in Japan without any further issues. The military provided us with what was known as "cola"—a cost of living allowance—that provided us with extra money to adjust to residing in Japan, which was even more expensive than San Diego. We discovered the necessity of this right away, as our cramped 650-700-square-foot, one-bedroom apartment—for our entire family of four—cost an outrageous $1,500 per month to rent.

We had to make some major adjustments to adapt to our new surroundings. Not only was the apartment tiny, the layout didn't work for a family of our size—especially since we were accustomed to living in a typical American house. The kids shared the bedroom, while Chris and I slept on a convertible futon sofa in the combination living room/dining warmed by a kerosene heater. In general, Japanese furniture was typically more disposable and smaller than American, which made our shipped American furniture—including our oversized entertainment center—bulky and out of place. We had a makeshift kitchen that could only fit one person at a time and a two-burner stove without an oven. Suffice it to say, it's not easy to prepare meals for a family of four without a regular stove or oven.

The other oddity was the Shoji room—a space divided by rice paper doors with mats on the floor. Japanese people generally use it as a tearoom, but I decided to make it a playroom for the girls as soon as the shipment containing their toys arrived.

My family made do with what we had, and we learned to assimilate, despite our steep learning curve. We took advantage of a military orientation program that helped us understand Japanese culture—important things to know, such as tipping is forbidden—and speak some essential language.

Meanwhile, Chris served as a helicopter mechanic for his squadron at the nearby Naval base. I was able to earn a little money teaching conversational English to Japanese students. Although I didn't have a degree in education or any training in this subject, it was easier than one might think because my material was limited to just conversational English. My students didn't want or need help with writing or grammar, but rather, the spoken word because American idioms are so difficult for people who didn't grow up with them. Japanese is a particularly literal language, so many individuals there struggle picking up English nuances.

More often than not, I taught my students right in our living room. I would revert the futon bed back into a couch and begin instruction while we were seated on it.

I was fooling myself thinking that living in Japan— or anywhere else—was going to improve things between Chris and me. He picked up right where he left off with his perfectionism and criticism, which was all the worse because we lived in such tight quarters in a foreign country—and with the children always within close earshot of our heated arguments.

It goes without saying he didn't treat me any better when I became pregnant a third time. As the months passed and my belly expanded, it became increasingly difficult for me to raise the futon myself to prepare the living room for my students, so I asked Chris to do it before heading out the door to the base. One morning—when he was well aware I had a couple of students coming—he woke up late on purpose, so he wouldn't have time to convert the futon into a couch. I attempted to lift it up while settling Alese and Ashley, but it was too much for me in my condition and I couldn't accomplish the task.

I had no choice except to instruct my students while we were on the open futon bed. The students who came by that day were put off by the unprofessionalism of my "classroom" and never returned after that. I can't say I blame them. They were right. They were paying for lessons, and it was inappropriate for me to do so on an open futon bed.

I complained to Chris about it later, but he didn't care less about how it looked or that his selfish act had cost me paying customers and income for our family. There was no way to describe his behavior other than to say he was acting like an ass. He didn't like that I had a job and enjoyed it, so he refused to be supportive. Although our marriage continued to flounder, I refused to let it hinder me from living my life, being a good mother, or planting roots in Japan.

There was so much to love about this country. I grew especially fond of the magnificent cherry blossoms unique to the Japanese landscapes. I felt safe there while exploring with my children—more so than in the U.S. The police didn't even carry guns. Although Japan was well known for gang crime, those incidents were separate from the rest of society, so the streets were completely safe. I could carry money and valuables around without the slightest worry.

We went on many field trips, including to strawberry festivals, the zoo—which was highly enjoyable, although it paled in comparison to the one in San Diego—and many shops, where I bought beautiful porcelain vases. I wanted to climb Mount Fuji, which is an active volcano, but was too far along in my pregnancy at the time to attempt it.

Of course, we had to take handwritten maps along with us wherever we went. Americans banded together to create our own version of maps with landmarks instead of street signs because they were in Japanese, which made it difficult for us to find our way around. The only things I was ever able to identify without help were the 7-Eleven stores and McDonald's, both of which were in abundance there.

There was one occasion in which the four of us were touring around, lost and exhausted, with Chris carrying Alese some distance. We couldn't interpret a single street sign. We stopped to ask for directions from a Japanese man who was meticulously cleaning his car. I think he understood that we needed directions, but we couldn't follow a word of what he was trying to tell us. After a while, he gave up and insisted on driving us himself. We were hesitant at first—in America you don't enter a stranger's car, especially with two young girls—but we were so desperate that we decided to trust him. The kind man drove us straight to Chris's base without any difficulty. We were so grateful! We offered him a tip, which he naturally declined.

I made a lot of friends—both American and Japanese—while we lived in Japan. One such family was the Tharps, who hailed from Cincinnati, Ohio. Rick Tharp had met my Dad when the family was stationed in San Diego. He and Chris now happened to be in the same squad in Japan. His wife, Terri—coincidentally another friend with the same name and spelling—shared my parenting style and helped me survive my miserable marriage. Their kids, Leslie and Bryan, were about the same ages as Alese and Ashley, and they became close.

As far as food was concerned, I developed a taste for gyoza—dumplings filled with vegetables. I avoided eating sushi, however, not wishing to take any chances of getting sick from contaminated food.

Thanksgiving became something of a challenge. It's impossible to cook a holiday feast with just two burners. I was unwilling to sacrifice one of my favorite holidays and sought ways to make it work for us. The church at the military base was kind enough to allow me to use the kitchen there to prepare my family's meal. I cooked turkey, collard greens, and other sundries, and baked apple pie, sweet potato pie, and pumpkin pie—all of which I brought back to our apartment for our family celebration.

Unfortunately, Ashley's school, which was operated by the Department of Defense, proved to be a major disappointment. The student and teacher population was too transient; people were constantly coming and going due to their families' military situations. Students from all over the

United States at different academic levels were comingled, which made classes too easy for some and too complex for others. Ashley did seem to be happy, though, and managed to make a lot of friends.

We had a few other inconveniences. While Japan had something of a Jewish population (under a thousand), there wasn't a synagogue to be found in Atsugi, which meant I had to carpool with another mom and her kids to drive our children to Hebrew school in Tokyo. Interestingly, although Japan is a safe country, security was extremely tight at the synagogue compared to what it had been in the United States. We parked in an underground garage and had to be buzzed into the garage or by the front door.

Once inside the synagogue, we found it to be well worth the drive. It was a fascinating experience to see Japanese Jews every week at Shabbos services.

Not too long before giving birth to my third child, Nick—a planned pregnancy because I really wanted a boy—we were finally allowed to move into military base housing. Imagine our delight: Chris and I had our own private bedroom! Plus, we had a full kitchen. What a palace! To make us feel even more at home, we adopted a beloved Labrador, whom we named Seau after San Diego Chargers linebacker Junior Seau. The Tharps had already been living on the base and were not too far from us.

Nick was born on February 28, 1993, at the military hospital in Yokosuka, Japan. As with the birth of my other two children, things didn't go 100 percent according to plan. The main issue was that Yokosuka was a two-hour drive from Atsugi.

This time around I was determined to deliver a full-term baby through natural childbirth without any medications. I refreshed my memory and planning for Nick's birth by browsing through my vaginal birth after cesarean class books and pamphlets from the National Cesarean Prevention Movement president, as I had done for Alese.

After I experienced severe contractions I now recognized as back labor, we hit the road. I had visions of giving birth on the side of a Japanese highway, but somehow, I hung on.

On arrival at the hospital, the on-duty OB/GYN immediately examined me. I was already eight centimeters. She said that breaking the water would alleviate some of the pressure and make me feel better. Well, that was a clear-cut lie. Her action initiated aggressive labor right away, accompanied by excruciating pain.

"I need a break!" I exclaimed.

"There's no time for that now," the OB/GYN dismissed.

I bit the bullet and endured the suffering. An hour or so later, Nick was born healthy without any complications. I finally experienced giving birth the way I had been planning for eight years. Even Chris was there without a softball game to distract his attention.

I was filled with joy when they placed my baby in my arms. He was beautiful. Physically, I felt great having had no medical intervention except an IV and the actual delivery.

Nick's birth was not the only reason I was in the hospital. I wanted—and planned for—a tubal ligation (having my tubes tied). I did not want another unplanned pregnancy. The doctor believed I was too young to willingly undergo such a procedure; she checked and rechecked to make sure I was certain about it. Chris took this opportunity to try to convince me to change my mind.

"No, I want it," I insisted. "I don't want an accidental pregnancy."

The doctor relented and went ahead with the procedure. I had no regrets. Deep down, I was probably so adamant because I didn't want another accidental pregnancy with Chris.

The only additional issue at the hospital was that the OB/GYN gave me a hard time about Nick's circumcision. She wanted the pediatrician to perform the procedure in the hospital right away, whereas I insisted on a proper bris, which had to take place on the eighth day after birth per Jewish custom. I won the battle and scheduled a return to the hospital. The day arrived and once again we made the two-hour trek to Yokosuka to meet the rabbi and *mohel*[2]. On the way there we had a minor fender bender, after which Chris tried to back out of Nick's bris. Well, I wasn't going to have any of that and insisted we continue, which we did. The circumcision took place without any other obstacles.

I have some fond memories from the summer of 1993 with Nick and the girls. On June 9, Prince Naruhito and Princess Masako were married. We all watched the elegant national event—Japan's equivalent to Prince Charles and Lady Diana—on TV, which was mesmerizing. We loved it so much that we recorded it and watched it repeatedly.

The first part of the ceremony was in traditional Japanese attire; for the second, they changed into western style with the bride wearing a white gown and the groom a black tuxedo. At the end, the Prince hopped into a horse-drawn carriage and situated himself. The Princess followed him in with some difficulty; yet, her husband never extended his hand to assist her. As we discovered, this lack of male courtesy in such situations was cultural and not unique to the Prince.

The Japanese people we encountered were remarkably warm and friendly to my family. Everyone adored Nick and the girls. They even gave him an endearing nickname—Nickochon—which we still lovingly call him from time to time.

Mario visited us while we were living in Japan. Originally, Rosa had planned to come with her husband, but something happened, as it always did, and she backed out.

---

2. The professional who performs the actual circumcision.

Mario spent time with Nick, the newborn, and the girls were thrilled to see him.

On another occasion, my Mom also visited us. She toured around, met my Japanese students, and spent plenty of quality time with her grandchildren.

Although we were in a bigger home, enjoyed living in Japan, and things were generally going well for the five of us, Chris and I remained in a bad place. He was nasty and treated me with disrespect, while I defended myself with continuous sarcasm.

During one of our heated arguments, he had the nerve to say to me, "If you would just be quiet, we wouldn't argue so much."

Be quiet? How can I be silent when we have three kids in a foreign country, and he constantly attempts to get a rise out of me by making demeaning comments?

I responded by saying, "Well, don't hold your breath of that ever happening."

We faced the fact that we were once again in desperate need of marital counseling. (Or, should I say *continual* need...) The military base offered us sessions with a therapist from its Family Services program. As before, this helped us only for a short period. I was coming around to facing the fact that nothing was going to salvage our marriage. We were a lost cause. We fought all the time about everything: *where* we were going, *when* we were going, with *whom* we were going...you name it.

I considered abandoning Chris and sneaking back to America with the kids. But then I asked myself: *How would that work?*

Terri joined me to confidentially check with Family Services on what might happen if I were to attempt to do this. Would the Navy send our belongings and cover the cost? The answer from Family Services was a definitive "No"; the Navy would not foot the bill to return our belongings without their service member's involvement.

The idea soared right out the window. I couldn't follow through on this if Chris were to be involved, as he would have fought it and made my life miserable. Not to mention the fact that I didn't have the financial means to hop on a plane, ship my possessions, and escape with three kids.

Even if I could have found a way to get out of the country, my family would have had absolutely nothing on arrival in America. I was stuck. I resigned myself to holding on for as long as I possibly could.

I had no idea that "holding on" was going to end up referring to something different entirely. On July 12, 1993, the Hokkaido Earthquake, which registered 7.7 magnitude on the Richter scale, shook Japan.

Our home trembled and swayed, and I immediately knew what was happening. I scurried from the living room to the kids' bedroom to ensure their safety. Along the way I noticed that our massive oak entertainment center was dangerously rocking back and forth; Chris was reclining on the couch, not realizing he was directly in harm's way.

I would never have done any physical harm to anyone, but I admit that for a long time I had secretly been wishing Chris would just disappear, so I could be set free. Maybe a tragic accident would befall him. Or he might fall in love with someone else and run off with her? I would have been perfectly fine with either scenario.

As I gazed the swaying entertainment center, I prayed: *Might it please just tip a few inches more and topple over onto Chris's head?*

The above "tragedy" didn't happen, but I still took it as a sign. How could I live with someone about whom I kept such bitter, morbid thoughts?

I knew that when we returned to the United States. I was going to have to find some way to terminate this toxic marriage. I had accepted the fact that it was doing far more harm than good to our kids.

Then Chris and I had our first physical altercation, which was only a tiny glimpse into what was yet to come.

Chapter Six

THICK SKIN
San Diego, CA: May 1994-Jacksonville, FL, December 1996

After three years, Chris's Naval service in Atsugi came to an end, and we were obligated to return to the United States for him to be reassigned. We preferred to remain in Japan longer, but, without an open position for Chris in his squadron, there was no option available for us except to move.

Yet again the military arrived and efficiently packed us up. We bid farewell to our friends and the place we called home, with promises to stay in touch. Leaving Japan was much more difficult for us than we had expected; the children and I loved living in that country, especially since Nick had been born there, and we developed strong attachments.

We deliberated for quite a while on where we planned to live next. Chris now had several choices of where he would like to be stationed, since he had served his obligatory time overseas. Though I was unhappily married wherever we resided, life was much simpler and calmer in Japan. When Chris was at work or out to sea, it felt like I was on a long-term vacation.

The bigger problem remained. I was pretty fed up with our escalating fighting and Chris's verbal insults. If I were to terminate my marriage—which I desperately longed to do—how could I survive with three children, no place to live, and zero savings?

I tucked away thoughts of divorce for the time being. I had to bide my time and put up with him for a while longer. I felt I was able to continue in our marriage by maintaining complete focus on the kids. I forced myself to envision a peaceful home life for us. I read books and magazine articles about how to create a harmonious marriage and home. My happiness was never a priority; I only cared about preserving an intact family for my children. I made it my mission to be one step ahead of his complaints and tongue-lashing. Occasionally, Chris took things out on the kids and behaved harshly to them—especially when it came to their academics—so I had to stay two steps ahead of him in helping them manage their schoolwork.

Ashley, in particular, had become fearful of his verbal outbursts and had begun to lie about schoolwork in order to avoid him. In turn, he punished her for lying by forcing her to eat raw hot peppers. On one occasion, her reaction to them was so bad she vomited. I scolded him for having enforced such an extreme and ineffective punishment on our daughter. His only explanation was that he had received such punishment as a child for his wrongdoings and had never learned any other way.

The immediate urgency was finding a place to situate, settle down, and re-acclimate to our homeland. The most obvious choice was for us to return to San Diego. But I didn't want to live there anymore. I didn't wish to again end up beholden to my Mom or my in-laws for our living accommodations and other support, except for short-term needs. I didn't think it was healthy for Chris to rely on his family so much anymore. It was time for him—and us—to grow up and become independent. Most importantly, I knew someday I was going to find a way to leave him and figured distance would be better, since at that point our families' involvement would be relegated to visits with their grandchildren.

While I always dreamed of owning my own home, I knew that was out of the question in San Diego, given our meager earnings and savings. We searched for a place with a reasonable cost of living and a Jewish community that also happened to have a warm climate and a variety of home rental options. For these reasons we were attracted to Florida, and, when a post opened up for Chris at the Naval Air Station Jax based in Jacksonville, we leapt at the opportunity. I conducted extensive research to determine where the bulk of the Jewish community lived. After various calls, I connected with Rhoda Goldstein at the Jacksonville Jewish Center, who told me everything I needed to know about Mandarin—a community that housed a large and active Jewish population. I knew right away this was where we belonged.

We spent our first few weeks in the United States visiting family in San Diego to ease back into bustling American culture—which was something of a shock after exiting a subdued country like Japan. Seau, our dog, joined us, but was sedated for the flight to LAX. He awoke upon arrival in his crate while being wheeled on a cart up the exit ramp exiting customs. His barking echoed throughout the terminal and continued non-stop into the arrivals area, where my Mom greeted us.

Chris's dad allowed Seau and the five of us to temporarily stay in his apartment, where he had lived during his latest separation from my mother-in-law. Our children reconnected with their grandparents and other relatives on both sides of the family, and I was able to catch up with all my old San Diego friends. It felt like a good distraction for us to spend time with familiar people, since Chris tended to display his charming façade while in the company of others. As soon as we returned to the apartment, however, his true self emerged. He saved all his nit-picking and vitriolic barbs for when we were in private.

Chris and I had something of a blow-up around this time. It started when our neighbor stopped by and knocked on our front door. He was probably innocently trying to figure out who we were and why so many people were suddenly living in the adjacent apartment.

Chris opened the door and greeted the neighbor with a friendly smile, while I stood in the background.

"Hi there," said the neighbor, a bearded man in his seventies. Something about him made me think he was a lonely retiree—a widower, perhaps.

"Name's Grady O'Neill," he introduced himself. "I live next door. You folks new to town?"

"Not exactly," Chris replied. "My family is originally from right here in San Diego—but we are just back from three years in Japan. I was on overseas assignment."

Grady's eyes brightened: "A military man, eh? In Japan? I fought the war there. Air Force."

Chris clasped his hand. Men in uniform always have that special bond. "Navy. I repair helicopters. My name's Chris."

"Always a pleasure to meet a fellow patriot, Chris," Grady said, patting him on the shoulder. He caught sight of me and asked, "That pretty lady back there your wife?"

"You bet," Chris beamed.

"Hiya," Grady bowed at me.

"Nice to meet you," I said. "I'm Monique."

"Happy to meet you, Monique," he said, turning back to Chris. "You folks renting the place?"

Chris was taking a bit too long to answer, so I volunteered: "Renting. The Hotel Del Coronado was booked solid."

Grady snickered politely, understanding my reference to the Hotel Del Coronado—a famous luxury beachfront hotel on San Diego Bay that was light years beyond our financial means.

"We're renting this place from my dad," Chris cut in, not amused. "It's only temporary."

"Mario is your dad? He's a good man," Grady acknowledged, confident his questions had been suitably answered. "Well, I'll leave you folks to it, then. Nice meeting you both."

"Likewise," Chris said, again shaking his hand.

Chris closed the door and locked it. His cheerful gaze converted into a scornful reproach as he turned toward me.

He stared me down until I asked, "Something wrong?"

"What the fuck was that?" he demanded.

"What was *what*?"

"You know what I mean," Chris snapped.

"No, I don't," I said.

He lunged toward me and thrust me against the wall. "*The Hotel Del Coronado?*"

"I was just being friendly. It was a joke—"

"A *joke*? About how poor we are? How little I earn?"

"No, Chris, I was just—"

"You embarrassed me," he said, his face less than an inch from mine. I sensed that his hand had curled into a fist without needing to see it. "In front of a *vet*, no less."

Maybe it wasn't the smartest thing for me to have said. I knew he was sensitive about his meager earnings and our constant financial trouble. He didn't need the reminder. Perhaps it was an unintentional dig on my part, I don't know. But was that a reason to shove me against a wall? A normal person would have said something like "That was rude."

I just glared at him. I could see the girls were scared watching the conflict from a distance, and I had to remind myself to curb my smart-ass inclinations to protect them. I couldn't care less about what rubbed Chris the wrong way, except for how it impacted our children. Until that point, at least, I wasn't afraid of him. No matter how awful he treated me, I fooled myself into thinking that deep down he cared about our family and wouldn't physically harm any of us.

He jabbed at the wall next to my head. "Next time don't be so friendly," he threatened, storming away.

I decided to pop a video into the VHS machine to distract the kids, as I did every time he exploded. I was unhurt but felt dazed and out-of-breath. I remembered the time he'd flung my phone away and wondered why he sometimes acted so paranoid and volatile. I prayed for the days to pass quickly and a swift move to Florida, so I could figure out how to maintain peace and hopefully get out of this disastrous marriage.

If only I had found a way to complete my college education and build a sustainable, lucrative career and be independent. But I didn't have any regrets, either; I loved my children and wouldn't have traded being a mother for anything in the world—even if it meant putting up with Chris's outbursts, which seemed manageable...so far, at least.

***

The remaining weeks in San Diego passed without further incident, and we headed off to sunny Florida. We found temporary residence renting a ranch house on Crosstie Road in Jacksonville that permitted dogs. Although the home was only 1,920 square feet, it felt like a good-sized home for us as it had three bedrooms, two baths, a living room, a family room with a fireplace, and a dining room. Returning from Japan, we didn't even have enough furniture to fill this house. The property was surrounded by plenty of grass and had a spacious yard for the kids to play in. I was concerned that the rent was much more than we could afford, but the place otherwise seemed perfect for us, so we signed on the dotted line.

Shortly after moving in, I went to the Jacksonville Jewish Center to meet Rhoda in person and to inquire about synagogue membership and Hebrew school for the kids. I had a pleasant introductory conversation with Isabel Balotin, the executive director, who struck me as a well-dressed, confident woman in her early fifties.

She got right to the point during my tour of the building. There were numerous offices, a large well-stocked Sisterhood gift shop, and catering for the attached Solomon Schechter Day School (which served hot lunches daily), and multiple meeting rooms surrounding the large circular sanctuary.

When the tour completed and we sat down in her office, she asked me an unusual question: "Are you planning to work?"

At first I didn't know how to answer her. Was it a trick question? Of course, I *wanted* to work and *hoped* to find a job—there was no way we could survive on Chris's salary alone—but I wasn't sure what I was qualified to do at this point. I had been away for so long—ages, it seemed. I had taught English in Japan, but that hardly seemed like a realistic career path for me in the United States. Could I resume being a phlebotomist? Was that even something I wanted to do again?

"Yes," I finally answered. "Why do you ask?"

"Oh, I just figured as much, since your husband is in the service," she replied. "I know the military doesn't pay well. Perhaps I can be of help."

She was being a bit forward, which I didn't mind a single bit. When she said she could "help," I knew she meant she had something specific in mind for me. A *job*. Now she was speaking my language!

"That's the truth," I leadingly concurred. "And our new place is pretty expensive. I'm hoping I can find something nearby that has somewhat flexible hours, so I can be available for my kids."

"Do I have the perfect opportunity for you!" she exclaimed.

My eyes widened. "You do? Really? What is it?"

"The rabbi needs a new secretary," she explained. "You would have the kids right here with you in the same building all day. We have preschool, elementary, and middle school."

I could hardly contain my excitement. I would have taken *any* job at that point, but I truly relished the idea of working in a synagogue. Maybe there would be a whole new career path for me in this, I thought. It's just a secretarial role, but who knows what it might lead to? Plus, I would be near my kids when they were in Hebrew school classes, which made it much easier for me to transport them back and forth. It sounded too good to be true. "It sounds wonderful," I responded, wondering if a shoe was about to drop. "If I may ask, what happened to the last secretary?"

Isabel lowered her head to conceal a smirk. "*Welllll*," she stammered. "She only lasted a couple of weeks. Let's say it wasn't the best fit."

I could sense something was off. "What about the ones before her?"

"They weren't such good fits, either," Isabel sighed.

I could tell the other shoe was weighing a ton in her hand; it seemed like a construction worker's boot was about to hit the ground. She realized she wasn't doing a good job concealing whatever issue existed and couldn't hold onto the shoe any longer. "I'll give it to you straight, Monique, since you seem like a good person," she relented, adding: "And *thick-skinned.*"

Why is thick skin necessary to work as a secretary at a synagogue? What is so terrible about this rabbi?

"Let me explain," she swallowed. "The rabbi is wonderful with the congregation. He's a knowledgeable, brilliant man, and we are blessed to have him. But he's not the easiest man to work for, if you know what I mean. Others couldn't tolerate working with him for very long. He can be quite…demanding and critical."

Demanding? Critical? No problem! Not for me, anyway. No one knows more about how to deal with someone with these attributes than I do. Working for a difficult rabbi can't possibly be as challenging as being married to Chris.

"I'm pretty sure I can manage," I convinced her.

I met with the rabbi and, sure enough, won the job. I was thrilled to be earning a paycheck and especially proud to be employed in a Jewish environment. It didn't take long for me to realize what Isabel had meant with her assessment of the rabbi. He was indeed a brilliant man but, as Isabel indicated, not exactly the warmest soul. Even so, I learned a tremendous amount from him. My "thick skin" came in handy on multiple occasions, as I was able to hold my own in conversations with him and stand up for myself when he wrongly accused me of making a mistake. Ultimately, I would end up outlasting any other secretary who had worked for him.

One of the many welcoming families we met upon acclimating ourselves at the Jacksonville Jewish Center was Beth and Mark Shorstein. Ashley became fast friends with their daughter, Rebecca. On one occasion Beth generously invited us for Shabbos dinner. Chris didn't attend, but the kids and I did. We had a wonderful time without him. Our invites from within the Jewish community continued—typically without my husband present—as one would expect from such a tight-knit active shul that had the added charm of southern hospitality.

Although it was good that Chris and I were once again a two-income family, our combined salaries still weren't enough to sustain us. We were never able to pay our bills on time—anything and everything was always late. There was never enough money to go around for food, kids' activities, books, sports equipment, braces, glasses, and tuition for three children to attend Solomon Schechter Day School—even though it was greatly reduced, due to our financial situation and my employment at the synagogue. No matter what bill was overdue, I always preferred for a check to bounce than for the kids to go without something they needed. I refused to deprive them in any way.

Needless to say, this caused even more tension and arguments with Chris, and we had a second "phone incident." Once again, I thought I had the house to myself and could chat away freely with a friend. The kids were out playing with friends and Chris was at work—or so I thought.

I recall that I was reminiscing about *happy times* without Chris and not complaining about him in the slightest bit. I must have been babbling on for some time when I heard Chris interrupt me: "How happy are you?"

Yet again he had found a way to sneak up on me. He stood in the doorway, glowering. Whatever was on his mind, I knew he meant business. I had to deal with him right away, especially after what he said next: "You know, O.J. got away with it."

His reference sent chills up and down my spine. It was the mid-1990s and the O.J. Simpson trial for allegedly murdering his ex-wife, Nicole Brown, and Ron Goldman was fresh on everyone's mind. You couldn't escape the constant barrage of news about the crime of the century, as it was all over the newspaper headlines and front and center on television 24/7. There was only one reason Chris was conjuring the image of O.J. Simpson.

After a couple of seconds, I was able to collect my thoughts, calm my nerves, and casually say to my friend on the phone: "I'm so sorry, but Chris just got home. I'll talk to you later. Bye."

By the time I hung up, he'd already stepped away. When I saw him next, I asked him to repeat what he had said—and *he did.*

I reminded him, "O.J. had money and you do not." It was unsettling, to say the least, but I tried to act blasé.

His sudden appearance and comment were clear-cut threats, and they stuck with me. Even though he made such a horrible reference, I never believed he meant it. No one would do such a thing, I thought. Those stories happened to other people, never to anyone I knew.

Not long after the incident, Chris went out to sea in the Mediterranean, with the ship docking at various ports. It didn't happen a moment too soon. While he was away, I began to formulate my "exit strategy." I couldn't take it anymore. I feared he was on the verge of a major violent outburst, and I didn't want our kids or me to bear the brunt of it.

As always, money was my biggest issue. I had to earn and squirrel away every penny I possibly could. In addition to working for the rabbi, I took on a second job at Stein Mart department store. Not only did it help make ends meet, my employment provided a discount to help provide the kids and me with necessities.

But Chris came back before I knew it. I hadn't had enough time to cobble money together and figure out a plan. The kids were always excited to see him, and I adjusted with trepidation. From past experiences, I knew all too well that the novelty of his return was always short-lived.

We certainly never agreed on how to handle the kids' discipline. I was unsuccessful convincing him that threats, scoldings, and punishments were ineffective.

As the kids grew older, the homework loads increased with Hebrew added as a dual language and half their days spent in secular studies. It was a major adjustment for Ashley as she had the least consistent education of my older children in Japan. Ashley swam on the Bolles School Sharks team and loved it. But when her grades declined, Chris punished her by forbidding competitive swimming. He would place her on this restriction for six weeks at a time. Unsurprisingly, this was not an effective tactic; her grades stayed the same, but now she was also miserable and not getting the exercise and training she needed. I found myself hiding her academic struggles from her father.

There were also signs of overreacting, bordering on abuse. Chris once approached Alese while she was enjoying some beautifully plump cherry tomatoes straight out of the container from the refrigerator. He snatched them away and reprimanded her: "Your mother just bought these tomatoes. Have you asked for permission if you could eat them?"

When she nodded "No," he spanked her so hard it caused welts to form on her legs.

Having heard the commotion I rushed into the room, grabbed Alese, and comforted her. "It's okay, pumpkin...."

I stepped up close to Chris and railed into him: "What the hell is wrong with you? You're out of control. That was completely unnecessary."

Chris was also occasionally cruel to Seau. Once he yanked him up by his collar connected to a leash and suspended him in the air because he was misbehaving. I screamed at him to let the dog go. The kids were traumatized by seeing their beloved pup hurt in such fashion.

All these incidents built up to a third, more serious physical altercation between the two of us.

I knew something was amiss one evening when Chris ushered the kids out of the living room in order to play a voicemail for both of us to hear in private. A deep, unfamiliar voice filled the room: "Chris, this is your commanding officer, Commander Franks. I regret bothering you about this at home, but I've been receiving several disturbing phone calls from various institutions that claim you are late with payments.... One was from your landlord about your rent being overdue. Another from a car dealership about a payment on your wife's station wagon. I would rather not be involved in your financial problems, but I have to deal with this because these folks keep contacting the command. Please stop by my office at 8 o'clock, and we'll talk this through. Thank you."

The machine bleeped, and we remained silent as we absorbed the message. I was about to say something gentle to him along the lines of "Okay, let's try to figure this out" when he flipped his lid. Chris could not tolerate that our financial woes were being made public, and I could tell he felt particularly humiliated that the military—his own CO, no less—had been dragged into this. Somehow, I was at fault for all of it.

"What the fuck are we going to do?!" he spat, slamming his hand down on the end table. "We're *flat broke*. We can't pay these bills now. What am I supposed to say to the Commander tomorrow?"

"I don't know," I murmured. "Let's try to stay calm...."

"Stay calm? Are you fucking kidding me? This is *your fault*. You go around spending all of our money on our kids—Jewish day school, synagogue dues, and all that other crap—"

His words lured me into a combative mode I didn't want. He had challenged my parenting judgment and my religious beliefs, and I wasn't about to tolerate it. "Don't start with me, Chris. I don't appreciate that you always insult my religion. And I'm the one who's always looking out for what's best for our children. You've had nothing to do with it, except for your constant criticism. Plus we don't pay the full amount for anything, and I always request scholarship and financial adjustments."

"If you didn't spend so much money all the time and properly took care of our household, maybe I wouldn't need to be so critical," he lashed out.

"Maybe if you made more money none of this would be an issue," I countered.

Both of us pointed our fingers at each other. He suddenly grabbed mine and twisted it so hard it swelled and needed to be iced.

In retrospect, I should have known better than to push this button. Especially at that moment. I knew he was sensitive about money and associated it with his masculinity and sense of self. My remark pushed him right over the edge.

He turned into a wild animal, his eyes reddened with rage. He threw me to the ground, pinned my arms down with his knees, and began to strangle me with his bare hands.

I tried to resist, but he was powerful and strong from lifting weights. "I wish you would just die, bitch," he grunted. "I could kill you right now like it was nothing."

His grip tightened around my throat. I couldn't utter a word.

For some unknown reason, he released his grasp and climbed off me just before I lost consciousness. After several minutes of forced breaths, I regained enough strength to sit up. I said nothing to him.

Then he was gone. No apology. No excuses. He left me to ruminate over how close I had been to losing my life with the kids in the other room.

I knew right there and then that this incident was the final straw. I didn't care about money, how we would get by, or what it would mean for my children not to have a father in the house.

I am done.

Chapter Seven

LIFE PRESERVER
Jacksonville, FL: January 1997-July 31, 1997

Chris left me no choice except to proceed with separation and divorce. Verbal barbs were one thing. Now, since our return to the United States, he was displaying signs of increased physical aggression toward my children, Seau, and me. Although he clearly loved the kids, his form of disciplining them was too much for me to bear. I wasn't going to put up with that or his physical outbursts for another second. I had finally come around to accepting the fact that it was far better for my kids to have no father around than one who might detonate at the slightest provocation—or any trigger at all, for that matter.

Chris must have suspected something was off when I silently rose to my feet from the strangulation. He was learning that things were serious, and I meant business when I became taciturn. I didn't rail against him or challenge him in any way, which, in some regard, is what he probably wanted and expected. Getting up and saying nothing turned out to be the best way to make him truly concerned about what I was going to do next.

He seemed tense—but not all that surprised—when I lowered the boom on him shortly after the incident, informing him that I intended to move out with the kids and file for divorce. He knew I'd hit my breaking point and seemed to take the news well. Too well, perhaps. It was unusual for him to accept a change to his lifestyle—whether minor or major—without a protest. It was as if he was making mental notes about my every move and everything I said. I somehow recognized that I had to be on guard, although I didn't know what for. He seemed to be analyzing my reactions...looking for any sign of weakness...*strategizing*.

For the time being, at least, we were able to cordially focus on practical matters, such as planning my move with the children and setting up Chris's visitation schedule, which needed to be flexible according to his work demands. While I didn't feel all that comfortable about Chris being with the kids, I believed he had the right to spend time with them and hoped to keep the peace, so I didn't impose any restrictions or rules except that the children had to be with me much of the time, including every Shabbos and for all Jewish holidays.

Naturally, the biggest hurdle was figuring out our finances. Our life preserver to get through the breakup was our tax refund. I filed a married but separate tax return. Chris and I agreed that I would claim two of the kids, while he would deduct our third. We would use our respective refunds for our own moving expenses and down payments. My share ended up being $3,003, which I somehow stretched out wide enough to cover the moving expense and a rental deposit for a residence at Coopers Hawk Apartments. I didn't care if I slept on a carpet. I was happy as long as the kids had beds to sleep on, food to eat, and clothes to wear, and would be able to continue with their sports (Nick with tee-ball and later baseball; Ashley with swimming), Jewish studies (Ashley with her Bat Mitzvah preparation, which was only seven months away), and dance lessons (Alese with ballet).

A few days after having seemingly settled things with Chris, he began to show regret and express a desire to make amends. I thought it had been too good to be true that he would let go so easily. It was becoming increasingly difficult to remain in the same house with him until I was able to move out. But I had to wait two months for my tax refund check to materialize and the apartment to be available.

One day he approached me with his tail between his legs and pleaded, "I will control my anger, I promise. Can we please go to counseling?"

I wanted to say something nasty like "Fat chance of *that* happening!" but I resisted the urge and toned it down a smidge. "No. We've tried that several times. The kids and I are always on edge. I just want peace in my home—and that is impossible living with you."

I could tell by his reaction that even this statement was too strong, so I brought it down another notch: "Maybe you will be happier, too. You might enjoy being away from me. Without the stress of our marriage, you might even be more gentle and patient with the kids. After all, you love eating pork and hate that we've been keeping strictly kosher. After we leave, you'll be able to eat whatever you want."

"All right," he responded, leaving the room.

His reaction was far from the end of it. I had a hunch he was up to something when shortly after that he offered to do some work on my Ford station wagon. We could hardly keep up with monthly payments much less afford regular maintenance on the vehicle, so on the surface his intentions seemed good. I didn't push back on him because my car was overdue for an oil change, and he had started to pick up a few pointers on upkeep from a friend at the base.

He offered to teach Ashley how to do the oil change while he worked. I didn't think it was in any way necessary for her to learn how to do this at her age and told him so. Was he trying to prove what a "great father" he was? Or was he intending to manipulate her in some way against me? I felt uncomfortable enough that I pushed back on him and said she could "go to a garage" for oil changes later in life, but he insisted and went ahead on the project with her anyway.

He and Ashley used a hydraulic lift and ramps to raise the car in our garage. After providing several step-by-step instructions to her, the father-daughter bonding moment ended quite abruptly. Either Ashley misheard or misunderstood something Chris had directed, causing him to lash out: "Go in the house—you're not listening!"

I heard a deadening *thud* against the frame of our garage door. I knew something had gone horribly wrong and ran through the house to find out what had transpired. Ashley was in tears as she massaged her head from an apparent injury.

"Oh my God, what happened?" I asked.

"Dad...slapped the back of my head," she cried. "My head...hit...the door frame."

I checked Ashley's head for blood and any other telltale signs of serious injury. I didn't see anything. But I didn't discount for a second that she had suffered a bruise and was in pain—both physical and emotional. "Go to the kitchen and grab an ice pack from the freezer for your head. I'll be right back."

I stormed through the garage door and assailed Chris. There was no "keeping the peace" when it came to him harming our child. "What the hell is wrong with you! She's just a child!... Always with the anger. You can't even teach without exploding."

Chris was never one to back down from confrontation— even when he knew deep down that he was dead wrong. But would he accept that striking a child in this manner was criminal? I was about to have my answer.

"Take your *fat ass* back in the house!" he fired back.

"You're no slim and trim man yourself."

Great. Now I'm insulting his weight. This is starting to sound like our typical immature jabbing back-and-forth. Is this what I am being reduced to?

My insult only goaded him further. "I hope you realize that after you leave here no one's going to want you with your saggy boobs and fat ass."

"These boobs fed our children—I'm proud of that. You worry about yourself!"

The dispute ended in a stalemate as I ventured back inside the house and tended to Ashley's wound and comforted her. She seemed to be settling down and not too badly hurt. I felt rattled and unsure of myself, though, ruminating about whether I should just get out of the house at that moment.

How can I escape without a penny or available credit to my name? I can't even afford a single night at a fleabag motel. Even if I could, that's not a safe enough option for the kids.

I hadn't yet informed the children that we planned to leave the house and their father. Was I prepared to explain this to them? I had to continue to bide my time until that tax refund finally showed up in the mailbox.

The next day, needing to get the kids to school and then drive to work, I entered the garage and let out a screech of anguish at what I saw. My car was still raised off the ground without the tires, but the rotators visible. The brake pads had been removed. The SOB had left my car in this sorry state as retaliation for my remarks the day before.

Naturally, Chris had already left for work. I had to call my friend Elaine to give my children and me a ride. I made a lame excuse to her about Chris "not having finished work on the car" to avoid having to explain everything that had happened. Even so, Elaine was well aware that he was manipulative and figured he had something to do with the problem. Elaine, the kids, and I ended up late that morning— all because I had defended my child and made a comeback remark to my poor sensitive husband about his weight. It always bothered Chris that I didn't care what he thought of me and that his comments never affected my self-image.

When things simmered down, I convinced Chris that we should sit with the kids and calmly explain our divorce to them. With our move imminent, I felt we had to bring the children into the loop and help make it as painless as possible. At the same time, I wanted him to know that my mind was made up. He needed closure. Once the children knew, there would be no way for us to turn back.

We tried to be as gentle and understanding as possible. Chris was at his best; there was no trace of anger or resentment, and he didn't make any nasty remarks.

Has he at last truly come to terms with all of this?

The kids listened intently and asked several probing questions. "Will we be able to see you both?" Alese asked.

This was understandable coming from Alese, since she was closest to her father at the time and too young to have been on the receiving end of many of his outbursts.

"Yes," I answered. "Dad and I will have two places. You'll be living with me, but also spending plenty of time visiting with him."

"Will I still have my birthday party?" Nick asked.

I wanted to cry, but held it in. My boy was turning four soon, and birthday parties are obviously a big deal for kids that age.

"Of course you will!" Chris and I shouted in unison.

"Will you be there, daddy?"

Now I thought he was going to be the one who might cry. There was a heart in him, after all. "Yes," he sniffled after a pause. "*Of course,* I'll be there."

***

Monday March 3, 1997: A day of elation and independence. My tax refund check for $3,003 arrived. I could finally move out and break free from Chris. I intended to put our relationship in the rearview mirror and make a *genuine* fresh start. Unlike the moves to Japan and Jacksonville, I would be making do without him this time. Naturally, I expected to facilitate arrangements for his visitations with the kids and anticipated occasions in which I would have to deal with him, but I was prepared to be civil and cordial and let everything recede into the past for the sake of our children.

I raced to the bank to deposit the check. At my next opportune moment, I wrote out checks for my first and last month's rent and security deposit for a two-bedroom home at Coopers Hawk Apartments. The grounds were beautiful, surrounded by lush greenery and featuring a beautiful lake with a majestic water fountain. The facilities offered tennis courts and a swimming pool. The environment felt spacious, serene, and, most of all, safe.

Now that the move had become real, Chris and I discussed child support and how we would divvy up our possessions. Everything turned out to be surprisingly amicable. He promised to provide child support for the kids, and he didn't seem to be putting up any kind of a fuss about keeping things I needed or wanted, including Seau, our beloved dog. Essentially, he claimed the heaviest furniture, whereas I took everything I felt would make my new home warm and welcoming. He held on to the sofa and the entertainment center, since he rightly pointed out that he needed some furniture for when the kids stayed with him. I retained the children's beds (which meant he would have to buy new ones), the dining table, and both sets of dishes to re-establish my kosher kitchen. I also packed up all of the items I considered my most cherished possessions: photos of the kids and all of the sentimental projects they had made over the years, such as pottery, paintings, and challah covers.

There was no way around the necessity of purchasing some furniture for the new apartment. Working on a tight budget of $150, I bought a sofa and chair; they were made of wicker and meant for the outdoors, but I knew I could make them work. After squirreling away some reserve money for healthy food, I used what little I had left to catch up on overdue expenses and pay ahead for the kids' swimming and dance lessons.

It goes without saying I couldn't afford to hire movers, so I rented a U-Haul truck to do it myself. (The Navy wasn't about to cover a move this time around, not for a divorce.) The night before moving day, I pulled the truck into the driveway to have it ready for loading the next morning. I entered the house and checked up on the kids' progress getting ready. I was pleased to find them in their rooms, excitedly singing and bouncing around as they packed their favorite stuffed animals and possessions. They were already starting to come around to the idea of living separately from their father, which made me feel optimistic about our future.

Then I smelled something funky. An aroma I hadn't inhaled in ages was emanating from the kitchen. It grew stronger as I drew nearer. As I suspected, Chris was humming a tune as he prepared one of his favorite dishes.

"Are you seriously cooking *pork chops*?" I asked, dumbfounded.

We never allowed non-kosher food—known as *treif*—in our home, and yet he had chosen this night—the one right before our move—to contaminate several of our pots, pans, dishes, and utensils with pork. After we had come this far to remain civil toward each other, was he intentionally acting out of spite? In my mind the answer could only be a resounding *yes*. He couldn't resist the urge to get in one last dig.

He cocked his head at me and smirked while continuing to prepare his dish. "I was just following your advice. You said I missed eating pork and would be happier now that I could eat it at home."

"*Uch*," I snorted. "You know I said that you can eat whatever you want *after* we left."

"Eh," he shrugged. "What's the difference? You're leaving tomorrow morning."

I said nothing and left the room. I couldn't get into it with him. Not when we were so close to escaping. I busied myself by packing other stuff and again checking up on the kids. But I continued to hear him humming joyously in the kitchen as he completed his dinner preparation and then consumed his meal. Once the noise ceased and I was certain he had left the kitchen, I snatched every item he had used to prepare his *treif*—the large cast iron pan, his plate, and utensils—and tossed them in the garbage can. I don't know if or when he discovered those things were missing, but I didn't care.

The next morning, Chris cheerfully offered to help me load boxes and furniture into the U-Haul. I figured that he had gotten his resentment out of his system the night before by sullying our dishes and cookware. I was grateful for his assistance, as working together we were able to complete the job in good time. We left the kids at home and drove off to Coopers Hawk, where he helped shepherd everything into my apartment.

He seemed pleased with his work and then suggested, "Would you like me to help you unpack?"

This might have been an innocent and well-intended offer, but to me it crossed the line. We needed boundaries and a concrete barrier from anything smacking of intimacy. I wanted the place to be set up the way *I* wanted it to be done and couldn't risk giving him false hopes that we had a remote chance of coming back together. Most of all, I didn't want to give him any chance to say anything critical about my décor choices.

"Thanks so much for your help, Chris, I really appreciate it," I said. "But don't worry, we're all good. I can take care of things from here."

He backed off, which made me feel relieved that I hadn't overreacted. I still needed him for child support and other things, and there was no reason for me to be hostile towards toward him—despite our past.

When we brought the kids and Seau over to their new home, Chris made his final farewells with hugs and kisses. I felt some sympathy for him once he headed out, but something compelled me to close and lock the door behind him. I beamed from ear-to-ear with my back against the door. The excitement of this new adventure was palpable. I had so many doubts that it would ever happen as the weeks dragged on, but now it had all come true: Our marriage was over, although we agreed to file the actual divorce papers later.

I had found a sense of peace. The hostility in the air was gone for my family. The kids were happy and content.

Good riddens.

***

The "honeymoon" of being a single working mom having been freed from a toxic relationship didn't last long. It became impossible for me to make ends meet. Although I had paid certain things in advance, other bills began to pile up: car payments, maintenance, and gas; the kids' school and activities; food for the kids and the dog; utilities; braces for Ashley; and on and on. By the second month I was already struggling to scrounge up enough for rent.

Despite his promise, Chris was not forthcoming with any child support money whatsoever. When I pressed him to follow through and contribute something—*anything*—he responded with more false promises. I didn't know whether he was being intentionally malicious, negligent, or both; whatever the case, the result was the same. I refused to allow the kids to go hungry or for them to feel the pinch in any way. Perhaps Chris was aware of this, and his plan all along had been to make me homeless or to have no choice but to return to him.

I had already left working at the rabbi's office and at Stein Mart for a full-time job in the employee training department St. Luke's Hospital, The Mayo Foundation. The job seemed to have greater career potential, but at $9.18 an hour (minimum wage was $4.75 an hour at the time, so at least it was more than that!) I wasn't earning nearly enough income to cover all my expenses on my own—especially considering my monthly rent was a whopping $679.

Heading into April I was reaching the end of my rope, unable to come up with enough money to pay the landlord. It began with a few gentle reminder phone calls to me from the rental office. One day, a warning notice appeared within the doorframe. Not long after that, a marshal showed up and personally served me with an eviction notice.

This was one of the most humiliating and terrifying moments of my life. With homelessness now a genuine possibility, I conceded that I had no choice: I had to get something official on record to coerce Chris into paying child support.

On April 18, 1997, without consulting an attorney—since I couldn't afford one—I filled out and turned over the divorce papers to Tracy Lee Cooper, notary and civil servant of the court in St. Johns County, specifying my physical custody of the kids but granting liberal visitation to Chris. She stamped them and put them in her To Do pile. During our discussion, Chris assured me once again that he fully intended to help. He implored me to withdraw the divorce and hold back the filing until December.

I foolishly caved and retrieved the papers. *Again.* To this day I can't explain why I believed him after everything we had been through. There was something about this man that made him seem utterly sincere and convincing.

Around this time, I had a friend named Pat who was now aware of my situation with Chris and offered to help out driving the kids to and from various activities. Since Chris was no longer present, she felt comfortable enough to visit socially and speak freely with me over tea. "I don't know if you were aware of this or not," she began, out of the blue. "But there was a period when Jack and I intentionally cooled off about being with you guys."

No, I hadn't noticed. She and Jack, her husband, always seemed like good and honest people. They had a new baby, and I considered all of us good friends. "Really? Why?"

"It wasn't you or the kids," she explained. "It was all *Chris*. Jack felt that his behavior wasn't normal. There was something 'off' about him. Something *dangerous*. He couldn't put his finger on it, but, whatever it was, Jack didn't want me and the baby anywhere near him."

The realization that other families had independently observed something "off" about Chris and had shunned us as a result made me shudder. My family had been suffering with him in both seen—and unseen—ways, and we had been paying the price with our social status.

For the first time ever, the word *sociopath* crossed my mind. I certainly wasn't any kind of therapist, but from the little I did know, I thought of psychopaths as deranged, cold, and calculating, whereas sociopaths are "hot-headed," manipulative, and deceitful. To me, he seemed like more of the latter.

How could I not have drawn such a conclusion earlier after having been married to him for so long, lived in the same home with him, and had his children? Now, being distanced from him and hearing this from a friend, it was all coming together—especially when it came to his lies about child support.

I decided from that point on to be especially cautious around him and not do anything that might provoke him. If anything, I acted ultra-supportive and positive to help him restart his life. I encouraged him when he mentioned to me that he had started dating other women. I even suggested that he continue to finish his bachelor's degree. He would then qualify to become a warrant officer and make a lot more money. He had already started college and was getting close to completing his coursework. Now he had the time to date whomever he wanted, study at his leisure, and visit the kids when it was convenient for him. I think he appreciated my support and advice, which made our interactions more pleasant.

My most pressing matter was figuring out how to dig myself out of my financial hole. After having been evicted from Coopers Hawk, the four of us packed up yet again and headed to the less costly Hunters Way Apartments on Arrowhead Drive. The grounds weren't nearly as fancy, but the apartment was larger and had bigger windows. Mainly, I was relieved that we had a place to live other than the street or back with Chris.

Meanwhile, I still desperately needed child support money from Chris. Once again, he tried to con me. When we met, he apologized profusely for not having provided for us and always tried to take me down memory lane. He had recently moved into an apartment of his own and said he was "just getting on his feet" himself and planned to help out all along but was having difficulties. Yet again, I bought it—hook, line, and sinker.

By the end of July, Chris still hadn't given us a dime and my checks were bouncing all over town. As impossible as it may seem, though, money was about to become the very least of my problems.

Chapter Eight

PROMISES, PROMISES
Jacksonville, FL: August 1, 1997-August 14, 1997

Originally, I had thought all I needed to do was extricate myself from my turbulent marriage and everything would fall into place. How naïve I had been!

I was eking by with lame excuses to my creditors and landlord about when I would be able to make payments. My Mom helped as much as she could when it came to buying a few necessities for the kids, but she drew the line at providing genuine means for me to stand on my own two feet. She believed—perhaps rightly—that I had to press the issue for support even more with Chris. "I told you that you could not afford to leave him. You need to contact the Navy and force him to take care of his family!"

I seriously considered her suggestion about calling the Navy but just couldn't get myself to risk jeopardizing Chris's military reputation and career. Plus, at least for the moment, he was acting civil towards me. I had a vivid memory of what happened the last time his superior officer became involved in our financial matters; Chris nearly twisted my neck off with rage.

As for begging for a handout or loan from my Dad... well, that was a lost cause. I was well aware that he never helped out anyone who needed money. I refused to give him the satisfaction of saying "No" to me.

Meanwhile, I had my hands full managing three children, planning Ashley's Bat Mitzvah, and working at two jobs: one, my part-time role at the hospital; and second, a new full-time position at the Jewish Community Alliance (JCA). Amidst all this stress, the last thing on my mind was dating. I didn't think I had the time or emotional energy to get involved with someone else or add any kind of complexity into my life. But, as the *Talmud*—the Jewish book of law—says, "Live well. It is the best revenge." Why *didn't* I deserve some company and affection after so many years in a toxic marriage? At the very least, being in a relationship would help take my mind off my financial woes and challenges with Chris. Besides, it wouldn't cost me anything. As another famous saying goes: "The best things in life are free."

My relationship with Barrington Walker, my coworker at the hospital, began rather innocently. We bumped into each other a few times in the hallway, where we made friendly small talk. Barrington was a lean, six-foot tall Jamaican security guard with medium-brown skin. Eight years my junior but mature for twenty-four, he struck me right away as well dressed, polite, and kind. He had started working at St. Luke's as a security guard after having completed a tour of Naval service.

Great. Another military man.

No, I didn't have a thing for men in uniform—certainly not enlisted ones. This detail was purely coincidental. There couldn't have been two more different people than Barrington and my soon-to-be ex-husband. As wound up, rigid, uptight, controlling, and hypercritical as Chris was, Barrington was well mannered, gentle, and understanding.

When we were on the same shifts, Barrington and I timed our breaks, lunches, and dinners to be together in the hospital cafeteria. We clicked right away, and I felt comfortable enough to tell him that I was going through an amicable divorce.

Later, my friend Rhonda—who worked in my department with me at the hospital—became curious about my choice of partner and asked, "Is he Jewish? I thought you wouldn't date someone who wasn't Jewish this time around."

She had a point. I did say that to her.

"No," I replied, "He's a non-practicing Catholic."

When push comes to shove, I suppose we all adjust our expectations based on a host of variables—timing, physical attraction, and need for companionship being high up there for me at the time. More than anything, I craved someone who would treat me with respect; a person I could talk to who would listen without judging me. Barrington fit that profile. It wasn't as if we were getting "serious" at this early stage, so I pushed the religion issue aside. Right now, the happiness of my children and me came first.

To my complete surprise, Chris offered something well timed: a chance for me to have a "night off." He volunteered to take all three kids that Saturday evening, which meant I would be able to go off on my first "official" date with Barrington.

I admit I was a bit hesitant to trust Chris with the kids overnight, given his history. I wasn't sure how I felt about them being in his home without my presence. But he was their father, after all, and it was inevitable that this was going to happen at some point. Chris seemed more relaxed with the kids when I wasn't around. Besides, I felt I deserved one night off and wanted to spend some time with Barrington outside the hospital. Of course, I didn't tell Chris where I was going, what I was doing, or with whom I was doing it with.

My first dinner date with Barrington was wonderful and turned out exactly as I'd hoped it would. It was refreshing to be out socially with someone who was delightful and upbeat for a change. There was definite chemistry between us, and we concluded the evening with a simple goodnight kiss.

The following morning, I called Chris to see how the kids were doing at his apartment. Almost instantly—without any provocation—he brought up the subject of dating other people. "I'm seeing someone," he leadingly informed me.

Well, la dee da! Good for you.

I didn't feel the slightest pang of jealousy. In fact, I was thrilled that he was able to move on. I let him continue, withholding details of my date; at first I didn't think it was any of his business.

"Her name is Claire," he blathered. "She's a pretty brunette. White. Real smart. She works as a nurse case manager...."

"Uh huh," I said, feigning interest.

"She has a four-year-old daughter..."

When he realized he wasn't getting any kind of rise out of me, he paused and then continued in a harsh tone: "You never loved me the way I love you. You never care when I discuss people I'm seeing."

Had he used the word "love" in the present tense? If he was boasting about dating someone else, why was he still speaking about our relationship this way?

"That's not true," I lied.

I didn't want to admit he was right: I didn't love him a single bit. "What I really care about is having a peaceful home. You couldn't be a nice person if your life depended on it. I don't trust you to be kind, it's not who you are. You still haven't given me a red cent in child support. It's amazing our children haven't starved to death."

"You're bringing *that* up again? I told you, I'll get you the money," he insisted. "It's coming, I promise."

I believed him less and less with each passing day and was becoming increasingly frustrated—so much so I felt an impulse to one up him. "I'm seeing someone, too. I had a dinner date with him last night."

He sounded incredulous: "You *did*?"

"His name is Barrington," I reported. "He works at the hospital with me as a security guard. A real gentleman."

If my choice of the word "gentleman" was getting to him, he didn't reveal it. If anything, he seemed to be neutral in his response: "Yeah—and what's his name again?"

I had no idea that, with this conversation, my life was about to change forever.

***

That Sunday evening, unbeknownst to me, all hell was on the verge of breaking loose. Chris inexplicably drove to St. Luke's Hospital, where Barrington was on his evening shift.

Chris waited in his car as Barrington made his security inspections driving around the employee parking lot. To this day, I have no idea how Chris had identified him so quickly. In any case, he watched Barrington finish his routine and enter the hospital before exiting his car and heading through the front doors.

Chris lost track of Barrington somewhere in the corridors. In a calm, cool manner, he questioned the front desk attendants—and everyone who happened to pass by—in the following manner: "Where can I find a fellow named Barrington? Pretty sure he works here as a security guard."

Yes, I had innocently exposed his name and job to Chris. In retrospect, this clearly had been a grave error. But why should I have considered this information any kind of big deal? Chris had been dating some woman named Claire—and other women as well. I had no reason to be suspicious, as I thought Chris had accepted our mutual desire to move on to other people and didn't seem to bear any lingering resentment. Why then did he feel the compulsion to confront Barrington at our workplace?

It didn't take long for my coworker to materialize. Right away he was bewildered by the appearance of this stoic stranger who was determined to speak with him.

"Yes, I'm Barrington Walker," he introduced himself. "How can I help you?"

Barrington extended his hand for a shake, but Chris glared at it long enough without reciprocating for him to withdraw it. He sensed something was off about this guy.

"Who are you? What's this about?"

"You know me, Barrington."

"I do?" he blinked.

"The name's *Chris*. Does that mean anything to you?"

"Uh, no, not really. Why should it?"

"Let me ask you something," Chris said, dropping any remaining sign of friendly pretense and shifting toward indignant. "Do you think it's all right to date another man's wife? Another man's wife who happens to have three kids?"

Barrington shook his head in recognition. "Oh, right. Now I get it. You're Chris—*Monique's* Chris."

"So she *did* tell you about me. Good. Then you know you have no right to be dating my wife."

"That's not how I understand it. According to Monique, you guys are separated and about to be divorced. She made it pretty clear to me things are completely over between the two of you. In fact, she said you were cool about it."

"That's what she said to you, huh," Chris reflected. "I'll give you the benefit of the doubt on that. But it's not the truth—far from it. We haven't put in the divorce papers yet because we're still trying to work things out. How are we supposed to do that with you getting in the way and disrupting my family?"

Barrington was not one to back off from a confrontation. "Isn't it up to Monique to decide on which guys she dates?"

"You *stay the fuck away from my wife*," Chris spat, for all to hear.

At this point, the nurses, orderlies, doctors, and another security guard who happened to be in the vicinity of the exchange turned their heads to see what was going on. Everyone could feel the brewing hostility. The area became unusually silent for a busy hospital reception.

"And what if I don't?" Barrington challenged him.

The men eased into each other, bracing for a fight but each one waiting for the other to make the first move. Neither flinched. By the time both seemed ready to spurt, the other security guard had joined the pair. "Everything okay here, Barrington?"

"Sure," Barrington answered. "My friend Chris here is just leaving. Aren't you, Chris?"

The two stared each other down—two broncos preparing for a head-on clash—when Chris flashed a grin. "Okay, I'm leaving," he shrugged. "But don't forget what I said."

"Yeah, whatever," Barrington dismissed.

***

It wasn't until Barrington called me the next day that I understood what had transpired between them.

"Monique?" blurted a deep male voice on the phone early the following morning.

"Yes?"

"It's Barrington," he said.

Ordinarily, I would have been thrilled to hear his voice, but I could tell right off the bat that something was wrong. "Hi Barrington—everything okay?"

"I thought you told me you and your husband, Chris, are going through a divorce," he said in a semi-accusatory tone.

"We *are* divorcing," I assured him. "It's agreed upon and will be in process."

"So why did he show up at the hospital last night and tell me that the two of you are still married?" he demanded.

"He showed up at the hospital last night? What did he say?"

This didn't make any sense. Why would he have shown up at the hospital? We'd only had one "official" date. Was it possible he was already jealous?

What is wrong with that man?

"Yeah," Barrington answered. "He said the two of you are still trying to work it out—or something like that."

"Work it out!" I exclaimed, becoming enraged. "We've *totally separated.* We live in different apartments and have already divided up all our possessions. I filled out the paperwork for the divorce. He insisted we hold off turning it in until the end of the year so he could finish school, be promoted, and I'd qualify for more child support."

"So there's nothing going on between the two of you?"

"*Less than nothing.* I'm long over him," I stated. "I thought he was moving on, too. He even said he was seeing other people."

"Why would he tell me you guys are still married and are trying to work things out?"

"I have no idea other than technically/legally we are still married," I replied. "He's crazy. Or delusional. Or both."

I took a deep breath and continued: "I'm so sorry he bothered you, Barrington. I had no idea he would ever do such a thing."

I could hear Barrington exhale a sigh of relief on the other end of the line. He was starting to sound somewhat more at ease and trust me again. "Well, I guess that adds up. The guy did seem pretty wound up and intense."

"That's Chris all right," I said through a forced chuckle. "He didn't threaten you in any way, did he?"

"No, not exactly," Barrington said.

"What do you mean 'not exactly'?"

"*Wellllll*," he hedged. "I may be starting to get paranoid myself...but driving home last night from the hospital I swear I felt like I was being followed."

***

Later that morning, through my apartment window, I heard and then saw Chris's car screech around the corner into the parking area. He wasn't due to visit the kids or take them anywhere, so his sudden appearance was something of a surprise—especially after my chat with Barrington. I went outside to give him a piece of my mind for having stalked him.

Chris seemed agitated as soon as he sprang out of the car. He raced to get in the first word. "Are you taking the kids to camp? Are you going to work?"

"Yes, of course," I answered. "What's wrong?"

"Nothing. I just wanted to see if you were taking the kids or not."

"I plan to take them, Chris, I don't see why—"

"I'm taking Ashley to camp," he declared.

"Just Ashley?"

"Just Ashley," he repeated.

"I guess that's okay," I considered. "But listen—I have to ask. Did you stop at the hospital last night and accost Barrington?

"*Accost*? I didn't *accost* anybody."

"All right, you showed up unannounced at the hospital and had words with Barrington," I said. "Why did you do that?"

"I don't think it's right for a man to date another man's wife," he explained.

"I'm not your wife," I insisted. "Not anymore."

"Yes, you are. We didn't put in the divorce paperwork yet."

"It's over, Chris, and you know it," I said. "You even told me all about Claire. Why is it okay for you to date other people and I can't?"

It was at that point that the kids showed up in the parking lot. They spotted their father right away and rushed to hug him while shouting, "Daddy!"

It had become clear that our argument was a lost cause while the kids were present. Not to mention the fact that it was late. The children had to be driven to camp, and I needed to get to work. Chris relished the fact that my accusations were being interrupted and gloated over his victory of having soaked up the kids' attention.

I threw up my hands in frustration. I didn't have time to negotiate with him regarding the driving arrangements. It was just simpler, for now, to concede to his request.

"Alese, Nick—come over here. I'm taking the two of you. Your father is driving Ashley."

The kids scurried to my car while Ashley seemed fine accompanying her father. I didn't have time to give further thought as to why he had so selectively chosen to drive her rather than offer to take all three kids that morning. All was revealed that evening over the dinner table.

"Mom?" Ashley asked.

"Yes, pumpkin?" I asked, swallowing a forkful of peas.

"Are you cheating on daddy?"

A couple of peas discharged out of my mouth like green gun pellets. *"What?!"* I choked.

"Dad said you're cheating on him with another man," Ashley informed everyone at the table.

"Did he really—"

"Yup. His name is Barrington. That's a strange first name, isn't it? Isn't it more like a last name?"

"No, it's not a strange name," I said. I dabbed my mouth with a napkin and asked, "Did your father say anything else about Barrington and me?"

"Yup," she casually answered.

Before she could continue, I inserted, "On second thought, let's talk about this later...when Alese and Nick aren't around."

"Okay..."

Sometime after dinner, I approached Ashley in private to find out more details of what her father had said to her.

"He said the two of you are having *sex*," she casually informed me. "*Lots of sex.*"

I turned livid. How could he have had the nerve to tell his daughter such lewd untruths?

I tried my best to compose myself. "Listen, Ashley," I began. "Your father and I are no longer together. We agreed that it was okay to see other people. I had one date with Barrington. We had dinner and kissed goodnight. I have no idea why your father would say anything like this to you. He is seeing other people, too—and I'm perfectly okay with that."

Ashley seemed incredulous: "Dad is seeing other people?"

Needless to say, Chris hadn't bothered to mention Claire or any of the other women he was dating. He seemed determined to characterize me as promiscuous and unfaithful to our children while he was the perfect saint.

For the next ten days, Barrington and I witnessed Chris skulking around the interior and exterior of the hospital at various hours. If he wasn't spying on us from a corner, he was zooming in and out of the parking lot the moment he knew one or both of us would be in the vicinity.

He also barraged me with phone calls at home. His mania seemed to be accelerating at such a brisk pace I couldn't begin to keep up with what he was doing or comprehend why he was doing it. "I want that man out of your apartment—or else!" he threatened.

"He's not here, Chris," I fired back. "You're acting like a complete lunatic."

"I don't want you seeing him anymore," he ordered, seemingly not having heard a word I said—or refusing to believe me. "If you don't stop, I swear I'll take the children and you'll never see any of them ever again."

"You won't do any such thing. I'm their mother and do everything for them. And I won't stop seeing Barrington—or any man that I choose. You don't own me. You need to stop making up filthy things about Barrington and me to our children. They are completely inappropriate things for them to hear."

I thought I'd stood up to him and held the line well, but it was hardly the end of it. The following day, I received separate phone calls from his parents and both of my parents demanding that I explain what I was "doing." I hadn't a clue what they were talking about until I realized that Chris had concocted stories about my lascivious relationship with "some kid" and therefore was "not a fit parent." Meanwhile, he portrayed himself as an innocent victim—a cuckold, no less—who was struggling to work things out and preserve our marriage while I slept my way around town. He had continuously phoned his parents and my Mom at all hours, begging them to "get me to stop."

I conveyed to all of them that there was nothing for me to "stop." I wasn't *doing* anything. My marriage with Chris was over. Kaput. We weren't working *anything* out. We were divorcing. He was dating other people and so was I. End of story.

After some effort, I was able to convince my Mom of the truth. However, I failed to make any headway with Chris's parents. They saw their son through rose-colored glasses and refused to believe anything otherwise. I didn't care. I was certain that, except for occasional contact with their grandchildren, I would not be speaking to them very often. After all, they were reasonable and level-headed people. I knew Mario and Rosa would eventually see through their son's exaggerations.

One morning during this ten-day span, I went out to the parking lot of my apartment building and didn't see my car anywhere. It was gone. *Poof!*

My first reaction was to call Chris. He answered on the first ring, as if he anticipated my call. "Hi Monique, how can I help you?" he asked in a chipper, mocking tone.

I didn't have time for niceties. "Did you do something with my car?"

"You bet I did," he answered. "I took it. It's mine. You can't afford to pay for it and my name is on it—so it's mine to take."

His logic was insane. Now he had *two cars* while I had none.

What a bastard. How am I supposed to get to work? How am I expected to transport my kids where they need to go?

Meanwhile, the reason I couldn't afford to pay for the car was solely because he hadn't been providing any child support. I deeply regretted not having finalized that divorce or hired an attorney when I'd had the chance.

I desperately needed to obtain some form of transportation. A friend took me to a nearby car dealership, where I found a reasonably priced and barely used four-door 1996 red Dodge Neon. I explained to the salesman that I was going through a divorce and Chris was in the Navy. I assured him that I would imminently be receiving child support from him. Somehow my negotiations worked, and I was able to receive much needed auto financing.

The car is mine—100 percent mine.

I giddily picked it up the next day.

Chris became outraged when he heard the news about my new car from the kids. He didn't waste any time striking back at me. He called my Mom and ordered her to "stop helping" me.

My Mom responded that she had no idea what he was talking about. He told her about my car and thought she had helped me buy it, which was not the case.

"I don't know anything about it," she said to him. "She must have bought it on her own…but what's so wrong about her buying a car, anyway?"

After my Mom filled me in on her bizarre conversation, I tried my best to process what was going on but could hardly come to terms with it. The more I tried to "keep the peace" with Chris and help us get past our marriage, the more trouble he caused. My mind raced to figure out what his next move might be. It didn't take long for me to find out.

Somehow I knew it was Barrington calling the moment I heard the phone ring. Before I could say "hello" he breathlessly shouted, "You won't believe what just happened!"

"What do you mean, Barrington? What's going on?"

His words steamrolled out; he seemed genuinely rattled. "I was driving on Philips Highway—everything seemed fine when a car sped up behind me. I was already doing fifty and the limit is forty-five, so I didn't know what was going on. The dude honked and flashed his brights at me, so I signaled and changed lanes. He switched lanes and followed right behind me, again honking and flashing the brights. I wondered if it was a cop, but then decided it couldn't be—it was the wrong kind of car, and there were no flashing red lights. All right, I thought, it's just some nut job—maybe someone who thought I'd cut him off somewhere or something. Or some wasted, strung-out kid. Well, I'd had enough of this, so I sped up to get away from him. He matched my speed and zoomed within an inch of my bumper—nearly rear-ended me. I looked in my rearview mirror and finally got a glimpse of the guy. I realized he seemed familiar. It was Chris—*your* Chris!"

"Dear God," I gasped.

I didn't have to ask him if he was certain about the driver's identity. I instantly believed him. And I was well aware of how dangerous it was to speed on Philips Highway; it was a wide, busy road with a lot of intersections and cars darting in and out.

"I'm so sorry about all of this. Are you all right? What happened then?"

"Well, it became like a car chase scene out of a movie or something. The faster I went, the more he floored it. We tipped *seventy*. I thought for sure he was going to ram me or make me cause an accident. I saw him in the rearview mirror grinning ear-to-ear. Like he was enjoying himself, having himself a real good time. It went on like this for several miles until suddenly, I looked again in the mirror and he was gone. Just disappeared. Turned off somewhere, I guess. My heart's never raced so fast."

"Are you all right now?"

"Yeah, but it gave me a major scare," he said, heaving one last deep breath. "Listen, Monique, we have to do something about this right away before it gets out of hand. First he shows up at work and now he's tailgating me, following me around. I think he's crazy."

I didn't want to mention my previous physical encounters with Chris over the years. Not then. Barrington was already worked up, and I didn't see any need to cause him further panic. Instead I said, "You're absolutely right. We have to nip this in the bud."

"Good," he said with some relief. "I think we should discuss it in person. How about I drive over to your place?"

"No," I said. "I'll go to yours. You've already had a traumatic driving experience, and you should try to sit back and relax with some chamomile tea. Besides, I don't want my kids to overhear anything we might say about their father."

"Fair enough."

"Okay, see you in a half hour. Bye."

After taking care of a few household chores and dropping my kids off at a friend's house, I drove to Barrington's place. He lived in a house with Mary and Vince Ponciano, who happened to be the parents of his childhood best friend. The four of us sat in the living room and—over some delicious appetizers prepared by Mary and some good wine (except for Barrington, who drank tea)—we talked through what had transpired.

It didn't take long for us to unanimously arrive at the same conclusion: To ensure our safety—and that of my children—we planned to file complaint reports with the police the next day to document the events and prevent any further escalation.

I thought we had come up with what was a solid plan to protect ourselves and put an end to all this craziness for good. If only it had met with success.

Chapter Nine

INJUNCTION JUNCTION
Jacksonville, FL: August 15, 1997-August 28, 1997

On the morning of Friday, August 15, Barrington and I sat in the Victim's Services waiting area at the Fourth Circuit Court, Duval County, Florida. I couldn't believe it had come down to this. We were really going to go through with it: filing papers against Chris, the father of my three children. But he'd left us with no other alternative.

I scanned the non-descript government room, which was packed with women of all ages and from all ethnic groups and socio-economic backgrounds. Barrington was the only man in the room, and I could tell he was aware of this fact and somewhat uncomfortable. The women struck me as somber and dejected, looking down at the ground with head in hands, staring off into space, or flipping through the available pamphlets on domestic abuse.

I, for one, didn't see the need to read any of those pamphlets. Why would I? I didn't feel like I was in the same grouping as these poor women. I didn't see myself as a victim. I was merely doing the right thing and safeguarding my children and myself. I was being careful, taking precautions, and hopefully preventing any kind of genuine harm from occurring. I thought I was being smart, strong, and independent and attempting to do what was best for everyone—even Chris, who needed to be stopped for his own good.

After an extended wait, I was jarred when I heard my name called by the deputy clerk—a short, overweight, and rather unkempt woman in her fifties who wore a stretched-out sweater that more closely resembled a smock. Suddenly, by hearing my name uttered aloud, I had become one with all these long-suffering women sitting around waiting their turns. I felt a smidge guilty that I was going in before them; if they had truly been abused and battered, they needed support right away. The deputy clerk extended her hand to me and, in a sympathetic but fatigued voice, introduced herself and instructed me to follow her.

"What about my friend?" I asked in a low tone in order to avoid potential embarrassment. "Barrington Walker—can he join me?"

"No," she answered. "I'll meet with him separately."

I flashed Barrington a sympathetic shrug. Not only had my domestic situation brought him into this mess, he now had to fend for himself reporting his harassment. Of course, I preferred to have his emotional support available beside me while going through this process as well.

The clerk led me around a corner, and we entered her closet-sized office, room 406, which had no decoration on the walls except for one of those oddball talking fish things they sell on TV. On her desk were stacks of papers, folders, and envelopes. From somewhere underneath that pile she extracted a tissue box, which she handed to me as an involuntary gesture.

"No thanks," I declined. "I'm fine."

"Okay then," she said, blowing her nose into one of the tissues from the box like a balloon flatulently releasing air. I was hoping she had allergies and not a cold, especially since I'd just shaken her hand. "Let's get right to it. Tell me what you've been going through in as much detail as possible."

I tried to condense my years of marriage as much as possible to get to the recent events: Chris's stalking, the manipulative phone calls, the threats, the car chase, and on and on. When I neared the end of the sordid tale, my eyes became watery, and I wondered whether I might need those tissues after all.

"So there you have it," I concluded.

"I'm so sorry you are going through all of this," she said. The line came out with such robotic precision I knew she'd said it to hundreds, if not thousands, of other people who had sat in this very chair.

"Is there something Barrington and I can do about it?"

"Yes, there is," she replied, extracting blank forms from within her mess of papers. She was disorganized and overworked, but there was method to her madness. "I have here a form I'll fill out with you. It's called a Petition for Injunction for Protection Against Domestic Violence. At the end of the document, you'll have a chance to choose from among the proposed appropriate methods of relief for your situation. You'll read over the report, sign it, and we'll file it with the court. Your husband will be served with a Temporary Injunction, and once a court date is set, you'll face each other in court, where a judge will make a ruling."

It all sounded so official, *so real*. A court date? A judge? A ruling? I truly wished I didn't have to go through all this nonsense.

"Are you ready?" she asked.

I took a deep breath and signaled for her to get started with the questioning. It began with the easy stuff: our names, addresses, Chris's occupation, his physical description, our current relationship, and so forth. Then came the biggie: *"Petitioner has suffered or has reasonable cause to fear domestic violence because Respondent has...."*

I had to fill in the blank at the end. Somehow it all came spewing out of my mouth: "He has been stalking me for the past two weeks. He calls me constantly at home, questions where I am. He calls me at work. On August 11, he followed me home from work. He has done this on several occasions, parking near my work to watch for me.

He has told my children inappropriate things regarding me and my boyfriend—constantly for the past two weeks. He was physically violent during the marriage. Nine months ago, he threw me on the ground, held me by the neck, and screamed obscenities."

The clerk diligently scribbled my words down word-for-word on the form. She next questioned me about our children, and I confirmed that Chris had, in fact, threatened to take the children from me. Lastly, we reached the section of the form that asked about "relief requested." I indicated she should check off these lines:

- *immediately enjoining and restraining the Respondent from committing any acts of domestic violence.*

- *excluding the Respondent from the Petitioner's residence.*

- *awarding the Petitioner temporary exclusive custody of the parties' minor child or children.*

- *awarding the Petitioner temporary child support from the Respondent.*

- *directing the Respondent to participate in a batterers' intervention program.*

- *prohibiting the Respondent from contacting the Petitioner in person, by mail, by telephone, by third party, or in any other manner; prohibiting the Respondent from coming upon the premises where the Petitioner presently resides or upon any premises where the Petitioner may subsequently reside; and prohibiting the Respondent from coming upon the premises where the Petitioner presently is employed or upon any premises where the Petitioner may subsequently be employed.*

The clerk directed me to read over everything she'd written for accuracy. It all seemed correct, so I signed at the bottom. She added her signature to the left side with the date and then stamped the last page with a *thud* to imprint the seal of the circuit court.

"Thank you, Monique," she said. "It'll take a few days for this to process, for your husband to be served with the papers, and a court date to be set. You'll be hearing from the court."

"Okay, thank you," I said.

She led me back to the waiting room, where Barrington peered up expectantly as if to ask, "How'd it go?"

"Fine," I assured him before he had a chance to speak. "Your turn."

Diana gestured for him to accompany her, which he did. As I sat down, I visualized Barrington undergoing the same process—the offering of the tissues, the explanations, the questions on the form, the stamping of the seal, and so on.

He returned to the waiting room sooner than I expected. I looked into his face to see if I could detect any sign of emotion. I'd hoped he wasn't blaming me for having to go through all of this. At first, he seemed lost in his thoughts, and I couldn't read him, but then he tensed up and uncharacteristically snarled, "Hopefully this'll finally stop the insane bastard."

***

In order to unwind from our stressful morning, Barrington and I went to a local eatery for lunch. We tried making light of the situation and cracking jokes as a way to release some stress, but it was clear neither of us felt any sense of enjoyment or relief. I kept picturing how Chris was going to react to being served with the Temporary Injunction.

Would he be frightened and back off? Or would he become furious and vengeful and try to lash out at one or both of us with genuine fury this time?

I felt a little better about things after having eaten, especially when Barrington suggested we take a little walk around town. He took my hand, and we made small talk while passing the small shops and window gazing. I leaned into his shoulder not only to demonstrate affection and appreciation for him, but also in the hope that he would draw in closer to me for emotional support. He welcomed my cue, wrapping his lengthy arm around my shoulder and kissing the top of my head. "Don't worry," he comforted me. "I'm sure it'll all be over before we know it."

We casually turned a corner when both of us froze at the bizarre sight in front of us: Chris was standing right there, a video camera propped against his eye.

"*What the...?*" Barrington and I simultaneously gasped. We still hadn't released each other and saw no need to do so.

"I caught you!" Chris exclaimed in a jovial voice. "I caught you both! I got it on tape!"

The whole thing seemed utterly preposterous. Why on earth was he continuing to follow us around, videotaping us? He was behaving like a child. A *lunatic* child.

Could it have just been coincidence that he was acting this way on the same day we filed papers against him in court? Had he followed us and knew what we had done?

Not a chance. He was way too giddy with the video camera for that to have been the case. Knowing Chris as I did, the idea of being "reported" would have made his head spin with rage.

Although we'd done nothing wrong, the video camera was starting to get on our nerves. We didn't want to be anywhere near him.

"Get lost," Barrington threatened.

"Chris, please, don't you need to be at work or something?" I chimed in.

He refused to lower the camera, pointing it up and down at all angles of Barrington and me, separately and together. "Nope, this is way too important. I've got you both on tape. I have evidence!"

Whoo-hoo! He has evidence: a man and woman walking on the sidewalk and holding hands. Someone call a police officer right away!

Barrington released me. I watched his fists clench and felt him tense up, ready to spring into battle. He was gentle and did not in any way strike me as a man who would initiate violence or look for a fight. But Chris was pushing his buttons. "If you don't get out of our way, so help me God—"

I placed my hand on Barrington's fist. There was no way I was going to allow Chris to cause us to be the ones to initiate a fight, which would have been held against us in court.

Chris chose that moment to stop taping and lower the camera. "All right, I think I've got all I need for now—thank you both very much," he snickered, heading to his car.

Barrington and I looked at each other in disbelief. Had that really just happened?

We decided we'd had enough roaming around town. We mutually agreed we should just head back to the car and get on with our day. Chris had achieved what he'd set out to do: spoil our moment.

No matter what idiotic things Chris was up to, I knew that at some point it would all catch up to him. I had the Injunction in my back pocket. I was just biding my time.

***

To my immeasurable relief, the court system cranked into gear, and Chris was served with the Temporary Injunction a few days later, on August 21 at 3:40 p.m.

Chris's nuttiness continued undaunted; he followed Barrington and me wherever we went, together and separately. I couldn't turn a corner without seeing him there—sometimes with the stupid video camera, sometimes without.

In fact, he acted out the very same day the Temporary Injunction was served to him while I was chatting with Barrington on the outside stairs leading to my apartment. Chris jumped out from around the corner and started videotaping the two of us. Chris and Barrington shouted obscenities at each other, and a physical altercation ensued. Chris shoved Barrington aside and thrust me against a wall. I escaped, ran upstairs to my apartment, and called the police. They arrived a few minutes later and broke up the ongoing skirmish between Barrington and Chris. A police officer searched Chris's car, where he found the freshly served Injunction papers along with videotapes of Barrington and me. Chris was cuffed and read his rights.

Unbelievable. I couldn't tell if Chris was failing to understand the severity of failing to heed the Injunction, didn't take it seriously, or was simply acting defiant. His parents bailed him out a couple of days later.

It became abundantly clear the arrest hadn't taught him any kind of lesson. As soon as he left jail, he headed straight to Barrington's home—where he knew there wouldn't be any cameras—and keyed his car.

Our day in court, Thursday, August 28 at 12:30 p.m., finally arrived: The interminable wait was over. The hot and sticky courtroom was not large, but it was packed with people waiting their turns to state or defend their cases.

Chris entered as he always did, coming across as cocky, well groomed, personable, and polished. He wore brand new, snazzy professional garb: dress shirt, conservative tie, gray slacks, and a blue blazer. He was accompanied by his 70-year-old attorney, Rudy Bolinger, who struck me right away as arrogant and full of himself, sauntering around the room like a prince in his fancy, blue Armani suit.

I rolled my eyes in disgust at the sight of Chris, wondering how he was able to flash new threads and this expensive lawyer when he had claimed all along to have no money for child support.

Fortunately, I didn't come unprepared, having brought a lawyer of my own to stand by my side in court: Daniel F. Wilensky, a tall, stately man with sandy hair and glasses. As it happened, his daughter and Ashley were friends who attended Kadima[3] together. A fellow congregant of the Jacksonville Jewish Center had recommended Dan to help me, mainly because of his at-ease personality and ability to get even the most contentious divorcing couples to find middle ground and mediate. When I entered Dan's law office for the first time, I marveled at a large sign hanging in the entranceway: "The ass you kick today might be the one you have to kiss tomorrow."

Dan proved to be a major comfort to me from the beginning. He reassured me that everything would turn out okay and not to worry about the divorce or the Injunction situation. I anticipated his legal bill was going to be hefty, but I knew he would be well worth the price. I also recognized that I had no other choice: I needed the best legal help like no other time in my life.

No friends or family members were present except for Barrington, who sat a few rows behind and not beside me since the court hearing had child custody implications that didn't involve him. My kids had just started going back to

---

3. In Conservative Jewish communities, Kadima is a youth group for pre-teens. After this, teenagers participate in USY, an acronym for United Synagogue Youth.

school, so fortunately there had been no reason to drag them into any of this.

"All rise for Judge Ruth..."

We all stood as Judge James A. Ruth—a stoic, robed black man with a thin moustache and short hair who was perhaps in his early forties—entered the courtroom. His strength and powerful presence commanded immediate respect. I thought he would make the ideal host of his own legal show like Judge Judy, who had recently become heir apparent to Judge Wapner, the retired star of *The People's Court*. Since this was my first real appearance in a courtroom, Judges Judy and Wapner—and maybe the cast of the original *Law and Order*—were my only frames of reference for what was about to occur.

We didn't have to wait long for our case to be called, since those who had lawyers present generally gained preference. Throughout the entire proceedings, Mr. Bolinger attempted to stall the proceedings by being disruptive with comments and asking for court continuances. Judge Ruth would have none of it and shooed him back to his podium.

The judge asked me to tell my side of what had transpired. From where I was standing—rather than being called up to a stand—I painted a consistent, damming picture of Chris as a crazed and jealous husband who was refusing to let go of his marriage, terrorizing the two of us, and weaponizing financial support as leverage against my family and me. I also described in vivid detail how Chris was trying to turn the children against me and was making up wild stories to them about my being sexually promiscuous.

The judge seemed to hang on to my every word and nod in all the right places. I became a bit concerned when Chris was asked direct questions by the judge; he presented himself quite well and spoke in a calm, low voice that was incongruous with the person I had just described. He struck the perfect note of politeness and respect as he addressed the judge, always mindful to complete each sentence with "Yes, your Honor" or "No, your Honor." I prayed he would see through him. Chris was a good performer—*very good.*

It goes without saying he emphatically denied everything and tried to turn the tables and portray me as an unfit mother. "I don't know why Monique would say such things about me," he stated under oath. "I have never followed either one of them, never videotaped them, and never came even close to threatening them. This whole thing is made up to get back at me for some reason. *I'm* the real victim here. I've been a really good father to our kids—even Monique admits that."

Incredible. His ability to tell such bald-faced lies with a straight face was right up there with the most delusional criminals.

When Chris stopped speaking and was sure the judge and the attorneys weren't paying attention, he glared at me as if to say, *"Take that, bitch."*

Judge Ruth didn't bite on any of the story he told, however. He had good radar for bullshit, no doubt having witnessed more than his share of narcissist, sociopath wife stalkers from his perch in the judge's chair. There was also the matter of his arrest for having violated the Temporary Injunction and all the accompanying evidence confirming my accusations of having videotaped Barrington and me. This was more than enough for the judge to move to a ruling and smack him with a Final Injunction. He read the first statement from the document aloud: *"The Respondent is enjoined and restrained from committing any acts of violence against the Petitioner. Violence includes any assault, aggravated assault, battery, aggravated battery, sexual battery or stalking, as well as any other criminal offense resulting in injury or death to the Petitioner...."*

It struck me as odd that any court ruling would need to forbid someone from physically harming, sexually assaulting someone, or even killing someone—all of these things are already against the law, aren't they?—but the word "stalking" made all the difference in the world to me. For the moment, at least, I felt a bit safer and protected.

He continued: "May the court note that I have also included the following: *The Respondent shall not make any remarks to the Petitioner or to Mr. Walker.* Do you understand, Mr. Rodriguez?"

"Yes, your honor," Chris said with his head lowered.

"As a result of this Final Judgment, I am also ruling that you are responsible for the forty dollar filing fee and the twenty dollar sheriff's fee."

Ha! Serves him right.

The sixty dollars in court fees didn't amount to much, but the fact that he had to pay them in full gave me a wonderful feeling of satisfaction.

"Yes, your honor."

That was not all. "I must give you fair warning, Mr. Rodriguez. This Final Judgment is serious and violating it in any way will require a very different kind of court hearing. You would then face criminal charges and, if convicted, incarceration. The bond for violating an Injunction is much higher for a crime committed when an Injunction is in place. Do you understand what I am saying and intend to obey the document?"

"Yes, your honor, absolutely," he said with convincing sincerity. The judge lowered his gavel to dismiss us and, without missing a beat, summoned parties involved in the next case. I thanked Dan profusely for all his help. Still, I found it impossible to celebrate. I may have "won" the day, but Chris remained free and out on the loose to cause more trouble.

His menacing gaze locked on to me as we all filed out, and I knew this ordeal was not over. I was far from done with him. A Final Injunction and all the warnings from the judge weren't going to deter him. Not by a long shot.

Chapter Ten

DANCING WITH THE DEVIL
Jacksonville, FL: August 29, 1997-September 6, 1997

The next thing I knew, I was embroiled in an all-out legal war. The injunctions and judicial warnings seemed to be backfiring all at once and just seemed to be riling him up even more. I don't know whether Chris believed he had any kind of realistic chance of defeating me in court, but, at the least, he probably figured he could drag things out, exhaust what little resources I had, and make my life utterly miserable until I caved in to the pressure. He may have accomplished these things to varying degrees, but I was never going to wave a flag and surrender. There was far too much at stake. Deep down he had to have known I would never relinquish my children.

Almost simultaneously after he was served with the Final Injunction, Chris filed for full custody. The divorce filings were most likely already in the works before that court appearance. If that in of itself wasn't *chutzpah*, he and his lawyer attempted to limit me to supervised visits with them. Chris knew exactly which buttons to press to cause maximum stress. He and Bolinger claimed that Chris had been the sole caretaker for the kids all along and that I was an unfit parent. The filing was beyond preposterous: on the one hand, they asserted that I was unable to support the children due to lack of resources; on the other, they had the audacity to demand financial help from me to help him take care of the children. I wondered how Rudy Bolinger was able look at himself in the mirror and, if he did, whether he saw his reflection in it.

For obvious reasons, I continued to retain Dan Wilensky as my attorney. He didn't miss a beat, filing several countermotions. The pressing matter was forcing Chris to pay child support, which his attorney had fought every step of the way.

As the legal paperwork swirled, Chris picked up right from where he left off with stalking and harassment at the hospital and at my home. Worse, he started doing "drive-bys" in the parking lot of my apartment at all hours of the day and night like clockwork at forty-five-minute intervals. He wouldn't honk, but rather, aggressively speed past my apartment with the lights off when it was dark. Even getting pulled over several times by the police for driving without his lights on at night didn't deter him. He didn't seem to give the slightest thought to the Final Injunction or to the consequences of getting caught violating it. I can't say whether his attorney was aware of his client's behavior or knew what was happening and was choosing to turn a blind eye.

Chris also barraged me with phone calls morning, noon, and night. In those days, it wasn't a simple matter for me to change my phone number; I needed my kids, their teachers, their coaches, and others involved with their activities to be able to reach me at all times at the same number. For those reasons and because I was in the throes of Ashley's upcoming Bat Mitzvah—which involved myriad details, including relatives' travel plans—I had to pick up the phone on every ring, even if nine out of ten times it ended up being Chris with some form of intimidation…

I'm watching everything you do.

I know Barrington is there with you.

You will never see your children again, I promise you.

The tactics were successful in that Barrington and I always had to have our guard up. Erring on the side of caution, he rarely stayed overnight in my apartment when the kids were home, and, if he did, he slept on the sofa. I would have never allowed Barrington and me to sleep in the same bed if the children were home. Yes, it may seem old-fashioned, but that's how I saw it (with or without us being followed).

On one occasion, after having a simple dinner and spending quiet time with my family and me, Barrington kissed me goodbye and trotted down the stairs to his car.

Momentarily, there was a knock at the door. It could have been Barrington coming back because he'd forgotten something, but my senses suspected otherwise. I didn't open it.

"Who is it?" I asked through the door.

There was a heavy breath of disappointment and a pause on the other side. My suspicions were already confirmed by the silence. I stood by, bracing for the worst.

"You can't fool me," Chris snarled. Without a doubt he had been standing nearby my apartment the entire evening. He had been waiting for Barrington to exit, so he could scurry to the door, knock on it, and make me think it was my boyfriend, so I would open it wide enough for him to gain entrance.

Since his attempt to get in had failed, he dove right back into his threatening rants. "You can't get away with it—you hear me? I know what the two of you were doing in there. You were having sex in front of the kids! My lawyer and the judge will hear all about it, and you're going to lose custody!"

I don't know what he was picturing had been going on that evening, but the kids had already gone to sleep while Barrington and I sat on the couch and numbly stared at a sitcom on TV. Sex was the *last* thing on my mind at that time. I chose not to respond to him at all and, once again, called the police. He was long gone by the time they arrived. They tracked him down and questioned him, but naturally he denied the whole thing.

The next day, Chris called to inform me that he was sending all three kids to live with his parents in San Diego.

"Fat chance that will happen," I countered, hanging up on him.

Not long after that, he called all four of our parents individually to inform them I was an unfit mother, and he had no choice except to take custody of the kids.

He took things even further by regularly picking Ashley up early from school in the middle of the school day for no reason. He would drive her around town in search of Barrington and me in an attempt to prove to our daughter that I was promiscuous and therefore unworthy of being her parent and guardian.

Dan Wilensky alerted Mr. Bolinger in writing that Chris was forbidden to remove the kids and especially could not take them out of state. It was getting impossible for us to agree upon temporary custody and visitation arrangements. Despite everything that was happening, for the sake of the children I didn't wish to deny Chris access to them— especially Ashley, with whom he was so close—but his attempts to brainwash her and his threats to swipe away the children necessitated that I take extra precautions. It reached the point that we had to do handoffs of the children at the police station; this was the only place where I felt safe and confident he wouldn't cause trouble.

The tornado of filings and complaints and Bolinger's legal shenanigans caused the courts to appoint a guardian ad litem (sometimes known as a "GAL") who would investigate the situation and determine what was really going on for the benefit of sorting out proper custody of the children. The $1,500 cost would have to be evenly split between Chris and me. It was yet another expense, but I thought it was well worth it if a court representative could see firsthand what was happening and end all this nonsense of Chris threatening to take the children away from me.

The guardian ad litem assigned to our case that visited my home one afternoon was Lisa March, Esquire, a woman around my height and age who had short frosted hair with a few blonde highlights. She struck me as a friendly, open-minded professional with a strong knowledge of legal matters. I offered her a cup of tea as we sat together on the living room couch, and I recounted everything that had been happening. She sipped her tea without any expression until I described how Chris "made his rounds" driving across my apartment building parking lot every forty-five minutes. She placed the tea on the coffee table with skepticism.

"Really," she huffed. "So, if we were to wait by that window and look out to the parking lot for forty-five minutes, we would see him driving through the parking lot?"

"Yes, we would," I answered without hesitation. "But it might be even less time than that, it's hard to say. He may have done his last drive-by a while ago."

Lisa took me up on the offer, and we hovered by the window looking for telltale signs of Chris driving around. She asked me further questions as we waited and then made small talk. About twenty minutes elapsed before Chris made his usual rounds.

"There he is," I casually gestured.

His appearances in the parking lot had become so frequent I suppose it was becoming less of a big deal to me. This was just another common daily occurrence.

Lisa perched closer to the glass; her eyes widened. She saw him, confirming my testimony. "Unbelievable," she murmured. "You called it exactly."

Lisa made some additional notes on her pad and collected her papers, stuffing them into her briefcase. Clearly, she had heard and seen enough from me to draw her own conclusions. I gathered she still needed to interview Chris, our neighbors, and a few other people before turning in her report. I prayed that having had a court-appointed eyewitness verify my claims would be enough to enforce the law and put an end to the insanity.

As it turned out, neighbors in various buildings were growing concerned about the drive-bys as well and reported Chris to building management. The manager took it upon herself to file a complaint with his superior officer, Commander Harry Storch. Apparently, up until that time Chris had managed to convince him that *I* had been the one stalking *him*. Now that the building manager had conveyed an entirely different story to him, the Commander was obligated to dig deeper into the matter. He brought in the NCIS (the Naval Criminal Investigation Service) to open a case and investigate.

All this activity seemed to be heading in the right direction and led to Chris returning to court to face increased stalking charges. Once again Judge Ruth presided. The facts and evidence seemed to be so incontrovertible that the Judge addressed *me* to determine the outcome: "What would you like me to do?" He turned to Chris with a pointed finger and continued, *"Because you are going to kill someone."*

By all accounts I should have said, "Lock him up and throw away the key"—but I couldn't do it. The timing was too challenging for me. As it happened, this was the week of Ashley's Bat Mitzvah. My in-laws had flown into town for the upcoming event, which gave them the opportunity to witness the courtroom proceedings firsthand. My head was spinning with all the details and the droves of friends and relatives pouring in, and I was fretting about what Chris might do to ruin the weekend for our daughter. Truth be told, I longed for everything to "appear normal" and for the day to be special and memorable. I couldn't take a chance saying something that might send Chris over the edge and risk Ashley's happiness, even if it meant putting myself in jeopardy.

"Your Honor," I blurted. "I just want for all of this to stop—for him to go about his life and for me to continue mine. My children need to be safe and can't be taken away by him. I don't want to cause any problems for him—as long as we are protected. Most importantly, it's my daughter's Bat Mitzvah this weekend, and it would devastate her for her father to not be there. I guess I have to give him another chance."

"All right, then," Judge Ruth reluctantly accepted. "I'll grant it to him. But bail will be raised. If he can't pay it, jail awaits him. I just hope I don't see the two of you in my court again."

***

Despite everything that transpired that week, the Bat Mitzvah took place as scheduled between September 5-6 at the Jacksonville Jewish Center. At long last, just in time for the event, my Mom chose to fulfill her desire to convert to Judaism, so she could fully participate in the service. The Conservative synagogue's tradition was for the celebration to begin with the Friday Shabbos service the night before, after which we had a family dinner—that is, my side of the family only—in a tiny room. That evening, I tried to bury my fears and put aside Chris—the stalking, the legal wrangling, and everything else—and focus exclusively on Ashley and my family. I wasn't going to allow anything to get in the way of this momentous occasion.

My favorite blessing, which I bestowed upon my eldest daughter, had extra meaning for me that night: *"May God make you like Sarah, Rebecca, Rachel, and Leah. May God bless you and protect you. May God's face shine toward you and show you favor. May God look favorably upon you and grant you peace."*

We awoke bright and early the following morning to prepare for the big day. I helped Nick, Alese, and Ashley dress in their new formal clothes, which my Mom paid for. As is the case with most Jewish families on these occasions, we spent an inordinate amount of time fussing on hair and dabbing a small amount of makeup for the girls, making sure they both looked their absolute finest.

My family made it to the synagogue without any difficulties and, as is customary, took the honored first row in front of the *bima⁴*. My parents and other family members sat in the row behind us. As I watched other congregants and familiar guests file in and take their seats, I felt waves of emotion throughout my body: *pride, excitement, nervousness, joy.*

It all sank in: *My baby is having her Bat Mitzvah.*

Then Chris made his appearance, slipping into the front row between our children who were thrilled to see their father. He was immaculately dressed, as always, and didn't show any traces of the madman who had been stalking and threatening me the prior weeks. If anything, by all visual accounts, he played the part of the proud papa. An outsider would have had no clue of the things he was capable of doing. Although his presence made me shudder inside, I had to maintain a cool and pleasant facade for the children and for my extended family. I reassured myself that this would all be okay, and somehow, I could get through it. What was he going to do to intimidate me at his daughter's Bat Mitzvah, anyway, in front of all these people? I had erred on the side of safety by not inviting Barrington to the Bat Mitzvah, even though part of me would have liked him present; I figured I shouldn't add fuel to the fire. However, just in case Chris might cause trouble, the synagogue requested that an officer be present to monitor him.

---

4. The platform from which the rabbi leads the service and on which the Torah is read.

As it turned out, the service was everything I had imagined it would be, and Chris was on his best behavior. Ashley looked magnificent as she read a *dvar Torah*[5]. Ironically, the *parsha*[6] that week was *Shoftim*, from Deuteronomy, which relates how Moses provided the Jewish people with proper rules of law enforcement. "The command to appoint judges and officials is addressed to the people," she explained.

Ashley explained that the rule of law is essential and must be enforced. Even in early Biblical times, community members were expected to be law abiding or face judicial punishment. The following words were no doubt lost on Chris: "Justice, justice shall you pursue."

Ashley led the congregation through the Torah service, beginning with the blessings before the ark. She continued by chanting a Torah portion and singing her Haftorah.

As anyone who has been through a Bar/Bat Mitzvah or has even attended such a service is aware, the preparation for such a day is arduous and stressful and requires significant time, patience, and practice—especially for a twelve or thirteen-year-old in the throes of puberty. Ashley was beautiful and poised under pressure, although I knew she was a nervous wreck over reciting Hebrew—primarily because of her inconsistent education over the years transitioning from San Diego to Tokyo to Jacksonville.

The festivities continued after the service with a Kiddush[7] and party later that evening, which also took place at the synagogue. Both were modest affairs with the synagogue and in-house kosher caterer providing significant discounts. Even then, I couldn't have afforded either without generous donations from family and friends.

---

5.   An explanation of that week's Torah portion.

6.   Passage.

7.   The blessing over the wine after the service is concluded. A luncheon is often served with bagels, lox, whitefish salad, and other traditional Jewish delicacies.

I felt immensely thankful that everything was going so smoothly. At the party, which featured a Mexican theme and was mostly centered around Ashley's eighth grade friends—perhaps forty in all—Ashley seemed to be in her groove dancing to everything the DJ played, including the line dances that were popular at the time. Nick and Alese had a ball, relishing the freedom to finally let loose on the dance floor.

My one regret was that we cut one too many corners by not finding a way to afford a professional photographer; instead, we had a disposable camera on each table and hoped for the best that they would be put to good use and turn out beautiful pictures. (As we later discovered, they did not; the photos ended up being lousy.)

The evening turned surreal for me when the DJ launched into the *hora*[8]. My family and all the kids whirled around with fervor until chairs were brought out, signaling it was time for the immediate family to be hoisted up in the spotlight. There is something thrilling as a parent to be seated in a chair and bounced up and down in front of your closest people to the rhythm of frantic Jewish music. All three of my children were lifted one at a time and then came my turn. I held on for dear life—you never know when you might tilt and slip off amidst the fun and chaos—I dizzily looked down and saw Chris beaming at me with his arms clutched to a leg of the chair. I snapped my head away to conceal my disgust.

When I was placed down, four of the stronger male guests braved risking hernias and raised Chris in the chair. He relished the moment, waving his hands up high and clapping with glee while everyone laughed and applauded

---

8. A traditional dance at festive Jewish occasions. Typically, dancers hold hands and move around in a circle—sometimes circles within circles—to the tune of "Hava Nagila."

with him. I had to exit the room to privately swallow back some food that was charging back up my gullet.

I would like to say that was the end of my brushes with Chris at the party, but it was not. He had to push the envelope. Later that evening, during one of the slower songs, he slinked over to me and publicly asked me to dance. I felt everyone's eyes upon me as I cringed and deliberated on what to do. Throughout the past several weeks he had been watching me, following me, videotaping me, accusing me, and threatening me with stealing my children—what could possibly have changed in my attitude toward him? How could he have the audacity to think I would want to dance with him?

He knew very well he was placing me on the spot and coercing me into doing something with him I did not wish to do under any circumstances. In his demented brain, he may have been thinking that this celebratory event had put me in a better frame of mind to forgive him and take him back with open arms. Or, maybe he was looking to demonstrate to others that he was perfectly sane—a romantic, even—and therefore incapable of criminal activities, which would mean I had been making up all those crazy accusations against him.

Whatever his motivation, he was aware that he had placed me between a rock and a hard place. He knew I would never in a million years embarrass Ashley or my family, and I was always diplomatic and respectful when it came to the sanctity of the synagogue, the attendees, and the Bat Mitzvah. I would never cause any kind of scene.

I swallowed my dignity and allowed him to take my hand while everyone gathered around and stared. I counted down each painful second of that song as we danced hand in hand. I ignored him completely and kept several feet between us as he tried to make eye contact with me; instead, I focused on my Mom and other family members I cared about in the hope I could block out the revulsion I was feeling. My Dad and Uncle Rodney seemed to be watching every move Chris made.

It looked like the kids were enjoying the music and games when, suddenly, I spotted Chris's finger pointing at Ashley and a friend of hers and saying something to the effect of, "You two better behave."

Really, *behave*? Everyone was having a great time. What caused him to assert unnecessary authority at that moment? He couldn't just let things continue happily as they were. I walked past him without any acknowledgment and ushered the girls back to the dance floor, thereby cutting him off.

I had thought the worst was over, but the most awkward exchange was yet to come at the end of the evening. As balloons and flowers were handed out, tables were cleared, and the DJ packed up his equipment, we fumbled out the door of the synagogue and tried to sort out the sleeping arrangements for the children: Chris and his parents or my parents and me. I had assumed the three of them would come home with me, but sides were taken on the spot. Chris—still in a jovial party mood—exclaimed: "I think the kids should decide—this is *their* night!" His parents thought it would be fun to join the debate and rallied behind their son.

"Let's let the kids decide!"

"That's right, we don't spend nearly enough time with them!"

"Okay," I rolled my eyes, turning to the kids. "Where would you guys like to spend the night?"

Ashley and Alese didn't hesitate: "With dad!"

"I want to go home with *you*, mom," Nick said.

I was thrilled to be with Nick, but I would have felt a lot better if I could have brought all three kids home with me. This was something of a letdown after the high I'd experienced from the day's activities (interactions with Chris aside).

"It's all settled then," Chris gloated, placing his arms around the giggling girls.

A few moments later, I realized Chris had collected several Bat Mitzvah gifts—wrapped boxes, packages, and envelopes of all shapes and sizes—and was stuffing them in his car. Now I had to draw the line: There was no way I was going to trust him with these valuable items.

I marched over to him and hissed, "What do you think you are doing?"

"Taking the presents," he innocently answered. "*Someone* has to safeguard them."

"And you think that person should be you? Nu-uh! No way."

I felt remorse that this wonderful day was teetering on the brink of ending on a disastrous note, but given Chris's history, I could not possibly allow him to drive off with all that booty—which belonged to Ashley. How did I know he didn't plan to pocket chunks of it and use it to sic his lawyer on me for more dirty deeds? Or just take the money and run off with the kids, as he'd been threatening to do?

Meanwhile, he had done absolutely nothing to provide for his children since we separated: nada, zilch, zippo. He didn't contribute a solitary penny toward the Bat Mitzvah, nor did he lift a finger to help me with any of the planning. All he had to do that day was sit back, play a part, and enjoy himself—without any of the stress I had endured building up to it, a lot of which was magnified by his behavior. Yet somehow, he thought he was qualified to safeguard Ashley's presents?

We stood deadlocked for several seconds, as our children and their grandparents looked on in anticipation of a looming battle. Neither of us trusted the other—and neither of us was prepared to budge an inch.

"Fine!" my Mom intervened. "Since the two of you can't seem to work this out, *I'll* take the gifts. Anyone have a problem with that? The two of you trust *me* enough to safeguard them, don't you?"

"Well...uh...yeah...I guess so," Chris relented.

"Sure, Mom," I agreed. "There is no one I can think of who is more qualified for the job."

Chapter Eleven

REASONABLE NOTICE
Jacksonville, FL: September 7, 1997-October 26, 1997

Now that the Bat Mitzvah was out of the way, I hoped my life would settle down and Chris would back off. He had no reason to hold anything against me. I'd demonstrated enormous respect toward him—far more than he deserved— and allowed him to feel part of the event, even though he'd had nothing whatsoever to do with planning it and certainly never had any interest in her Jewish education; if anything, he showed disdain for our religion and practices.

I didn't expect Chris to express gratitude for not having told Judge Ruth to throw the book at him while I'd had the chance, which would have meant spending the weekend and probably a lot more locked up in a cell rather than partying. I also didn't imagine that he would thank me for not having invited Barrington, for having tolerated his inclusion in the chair raising tradition, and for not having caused a scene when he asked me to dance. I'd sucked it all up and behaved diplomatically and with great restraint, although I certainly can't say I acted warm and inviting to him, either.

Not only was Chris ungrateful for my tolerance towards him despite his repeated hostility, he continued right where he left off with his erratic behavior following the weekend's festivities. Every day he plotted some fresh maneuver to rattle me. All of this, despite his parents' pleas for him to stop what he was doing. The children became pawns for his brainwashing games. Whenever he picked up Ashley or Alese, he would plant seeds about my "violating our wedding vows" and question them about my activities with Barrington. He made sure to take one daughter at a time, so there was always one left to "keep an eye on me" and report back to him what I was doing.

Nick, who was only four years old at the time, was too young to understand the concepts his father was attempting to implant in his head and couldn't offer any concrete information, so he was left out of the spy ring. Even this had a repercussion, as my poor little pumpkin felt devastated being left out while his sisters garnered all his dad's attention.

At one time or another, all three of the kids were subjected to a bizarre scheme in which Chris would withhold important possessions of theirs for no apparent reason. I could only speculate he was trying to wield control, force visitations at some later date to claim the items, or just wanted me to spend money out of my own pocket to replace them. He once refused to give Ashley her backpack when she forgot it in his car. On a separate occasion, he would not surrender Nick's new tee-ball glove and bat, both of which he needed for practice. It was yet another hassle for me to have to race to the store and buy a new glove at the last minute so Nick could play. Over time, Chris held on to articles of clothing, as well as Nick's Space Jam lunchbox and Toy Story backpack. I asked Dan Wilensky to contact Rudy Bolinger demanding that his client return the kids' items, but nothing ever got through to him.

That entire month Chris wreaked havoc on our schedules, showing up unexpectedly and trying to interfere with plans I'd made with the kids. On September 21, we were going to spend the day at the beach with a friend of mine. Chris appeared unannounced early in the morning, demanding that he take the girls out for breakfast. He disappeared with the two of them for several hours, finally returning at 3:00

in the afternoon. Not only did he cut our beach day short, he managed to convince Ashley not to join us at all.

In an attempt to have some semblance of continuity for the kids, I mailed Chris a written schedule of activities:

Monday: N/A

Tuesday: 4:30-6:00 Ashley Swim Practice

5:30-7:00 Nick Tee-Ball Practice

6:30-8:00 Alese Girl Scouts

Wednesday: 1:30-2:15 Nick Soccer/Sports Class

4:00-4:50 Alese Ballet

7:00-9:00 Ashley Hebrew High School

Thursday: 4:30-6:00 Ashley Swim Practice

Friday: N/A

Saturday: Tee-Ball Game (depending on the schedule)

10:00-1:00 p.m. Shabbos Services

Sunday: 1:30-3:00 Nick Tee-Ball Practice

When the schedule failed to prevent Chris from spoiling our routine, Dan suggested that he ask Rudy Bolinger to explain the meaning of "reasonable notice" to his client. He was also told through his attorney that he could not dictate to me what I was allowed and not allowed to do with the children.

The kids weren't his only method of attack. He called my boss at the Jewish Community Alliance (JCA) to try to get me in trouble and perhaps lose my job. I don't know what he said to her, but just the fact that he contacted her was sufficient evidence of harassment, and I made sure a police report was written.

Chris became relentless. On weekdays, he'd follow me from work to lunch. Fed up, I called the police and informed them that he was yet again breaking the Injunction. They found and detained him, but then released him when he made up a convincing enough explanation for why he had been near me.

During evening hours and well into the night, he'd continue to circle around my apartment parking lot with the car lights off. Either he would do a quick drive-by or search around for my car or Barrington's.

On one occasion, he called my home at 1:30 a.m. demanding that I wake the girls. When I refused and hung up, he called right back and threatened to ring the police saying he was concerned and needed to conduct a welfare check on his kids.

Next he worked on trying to get me thrown out of my apartment. When I arrived home one day, my building manager told me that Chris had handed her a copy of the eviction papers from my previous apartment. His act had at least some of its intended effect, as I now had to explain to her why I had been evicted. Chris's hope was to raise suspicions with the manager regarding my ability to pay rent, and then she would throw me out. If this were to occur, it would give Chris more ammunition to argue for custody of the kids.

Chris even took Ashley's key to my apartment and let himself inside when I wasn't there. It took me some time to figure out he had been in my apartment, and I was unable to pinpoint which, if any, items he had stolen. Either way, I knew he had been rummaging my things and had caused enough disruption to terrorize Seau. When I let him out to clean the crate, the dog was still trembling from fear. Apparently, whatever Chris had been doing, it made Seau so nervous he shit the crate. This was something that had *never* occurred before or after; he was disciplined and well trained.

During this time period Chris had an affinity for causing automotive damage. When I noticed that my car was making all kinds of inexplicable strange noises, I took it to the dealer for a check-up. After waiting for about a half hour, the mechanic came out and informed me that someone had sabotaged the car. I needed to have a locking gas cap installed because some foreign substance had been poured into the tank. The car dealer, who was aware of my situation, felt pity on me and placed on a new locking gas cap at no charge.

Repeated visits to the courthouse didn't accomplish anything. Chris always managed to talk his way out of jail time. How I wished I could have turned back the clock and had Judge Ruth incarcerate him when I'd had the chance! Now it seemed as if the courts were sick and tired of our frequent appearances and legal ping pong and were growing numb to all of Chris's behavior. He was having himself a grand time getting away with his criminal acts and no doubt laughing to himself at how no one could keep up with him as he drove us all in circles.

When leaving court one afternoon that September, he smashed the window of Barrington's Volkswagen Jetta to bits. It wasn't until a year later that I discovered what instrument he'd used to inflict the damage. The barrel of Nick's tee-ball bat, which had finally been returned to us, was riddled with shards of glass.

Even his own gold Saturn was not immune to damage from his recklessness. Out of the blue, Chris called the police to report it stolen. The police who investigated the alleged crime scene knew the claim was unfounded because they did not see any broken glass where Chris claimed the Saturn had been parked and hijacked.

By no mere coincidence, that same day a hit and run was reported involving two cars in the wee hours of the morning. Vehicle #1 came barreling out of Robinwood Apartments—where Chris happened to live—and struck a car that had the right of way, causing it to flip and roll. The driver of vehicle #2, who never saw what had hit him, suffered a series of minor injuries. The driver of vehicle #1 never stopped to render aid nor call 911—just sped off. The police found a telltale clue on the road near the collision: the front bumper of a gold Saturn.

The investigation into the hit-and-run continued over the next few weeks and did eventually reach some form of resolution, though not how one might expect. As it turned out, reckless driving ended up being *the least* of the charges mounted against Chris.

***

In the middle of the night on October 10, 1997, I was again awoken by the incessant ring of my telephone. When I picked up, I was not surprised to hear Chris's voice. I looked at my alarm clock on the night table and saw that it was 12:30 a.m. I grumbled and rubbed my eyes, knowing I'd be exhausted the entire next day at work. This had become my norm.

"I warned you," he growled.

"You warned me about what?" I asked.

"I warned you about *him* being in your bed when the kids are there."

"Chris, you're imagining things," I said in a monotone voice. "No one is here, I'm all alone. I don't know what you are talking about."

"If he doesn't leave, *I will kill you,*" he roared, slamming the phone down.

I couldn't believe it. He'd actually said those bone-chilling words. It dawned on me that beyond a shadow of a doubt my life was in serious jeopardy; no longer was this only a matter of him following me around with a video camera and smashing a window every now and then. Despite the profound effect of that statement, I could not imagine he would cause serious physical harm to me. Nonetheless, it was terrifying to hear. His pent-up rage was about ready to be unleashed. After a few moments of panic, I reached over to the phone to dial the police.

Just as I was about to pick up the receiver, the phone rang again. I steeled myself to get in the first word this time: "I told you not to threaten me, Chris," I warned him. "You are going to get yourself into much bigger trouble than you can handle."

"I said I am going to kill you and I mean it. It's not a threat: *it's a promise.*"

"Go to hell," I countered, hanging up before he could get in another word. I dialed the police before he had a chance to call me back.

Fifteen minutes later, two police officers arrived to take down the report. After questioning me for a few minutes, they called Chris up to check his version of the story. He claimed he had been sleeping and their call had woken him up. He denied everything, asserting that he had no idea what the officer was talking about regarding menacing phone calls to me.

The next day, I went to Radio Shack to purchase a telephone recording device. During my subsequent conversation with Chris, I informed him that I planned to record each one of our conversations, as well as those he had with the kids. "Be careful what you say," I advised him. "I'm recording you right now."

"That's fine—go ahead and record me," he counterpunched. "It doesn't matter at all. I'm recording you, too."

From then on, I felt completely changed. With those phone calls I had gone from being a stalking victim to a deeply paranoid person. I took note of every single car that was around me when I was walking in public. I noticed which vehicles were driving too close behind or beside me on the road. My senses were heightened; I was acutely aware of everything happening around me at all times, constantly on edge, and hypersensitive and jumpy to whatever unexpected things might come my way.

I remember having an ominous feeling while entering my doctor's office one afternoon. The hallway seemed unusually empty and silent. When I reached the elevator, I noticed that it was out of order and emblazoned with a haphazardly written sign directing me to take the stairs.

My mind raced to all kinds of paranoid thoughts.

Is this a ploy? Is he trying to lure me to the stairway and kill me?

Despite my trepidation, I compelled myself to walk into the stairwell and up to the appointment. No one was around, and I made it through the doctor's visit safe and sound. But even afterward I worried about how I was going to continue like this knowing he was always out there, potentially masterminding some diabolical plot to catch me when I least expect it and hurt me.

***

As if potential physical harm wasn't enough, I had another serious issue to worry about: keeping my job at the JCA. My status was already hanging by a thread, as I'd only begun working there several weeks earlier, and I was still going through the organization's standard ninety-day probationary period for new employees, during which time my personal life was already interfering with my performance. Given everything that was happening, I decided it was best to bring my supervisor into the loop about the stalking and the custody battle. I concluded that it was wise to be transparent and upfront about likely missed work hours due to my court appearances and frequent last-minute filling in for Chris when he failed to pick up one of the kids from one of their activities.

My job performance indeed suffered from the increased absences and my perpetual state of frenzy. On top of that, Chris had the nerve to phone my supervisor and issue a warning that he planned to "cause trouble" for me at work. This was enough for her to present me with a letter of termination. This was easy enough for her to do from a legal standpoint, since I was still on probation. My supervisor was not unsympathetic to my situation; she wanted to help but couldn't take a chance of workplace violence. "Off the record," she consoled me. "As soon as all this mess is straightened out, please don't hesitate to come to me, and I'll hire you back."

***

October seemed never-ending. Everything was turning sour and composting all at once. I no longer had a job or any money coming in since I had stopped working at the hospital a few weeks earlier and was now terminated at the JCA. The incidents kept piling up, and I felt trapped in a tape-loop episode of *The Twilight Zone*: first, the stalking; second, the arrival of the police; third, his finding some way to get out of it scot-free; fourth, repeat.

Matters failed to improve even when I had witnesses. At approximately 7 p.m. on October 19, while I was chatting with my neighbors—a couple and their teenage son—they caught sight of Chris crouching behind a bush on the outskirts of the apartment complex. Having seen him lurking about the premises before and knowing his history with me, they gave him chase. Chris bolted down to the street to his car, which he had left there at the ready in case he needed to make such an escape.

I call the police. I provide detailed testimony for the report. The cops find Chris and question him. He denies everything, making up a fresh alibi. He dodges another bullet. Welcome, you have entered my Twilight Zone.

After this latest fiasco ended and the police left, I realized it was getting late and I desperately needed to go to the store for groceries. I dove into my car and sped off to the supermarket. On my way there, I became certain that I saw Chris's car a few vehicles behind me. There was no way this could be chalked up to coincidence.

I parked my car and dashed into the supermarket, where I grabbed items at lightning-speed. While on the checkout line, I deliberated on my course of action. It occurred to me that if he was stalking me twice in the same day—including the first which involved witnesses and a police report— he would have no qualms about attempting a third time. I feared that by this point he had grown so desperate he truly was out for my blood.

At first I considered calling Barrington for a ride home, but changed my mind when I pictured the scene that would ensue if he were to again lock antlers with Chris in public. Instead, I summoned the police, who graciously gave me a police escort to my house.

Having arrived home safely, I put the groceries away and made my rounds checking on the kids. I kissed each of my girls goodnight and was surprised that Nick wasn't in his room. I opened my bedroom door and found him peacefully asleep on my bed. I watched my sweet boy for a few moments before joining him on the bed. My mind was able to relax and clear from the day's latest perils. I felt myself drifting off.

Suddenly, I heard an intense shattering of glass through my bedroom window. I grabbed Nick, fled the room, and called the police. When the officers came, they surveyed the area surrounding the apartment but failed to turn up any evidence indicating Chris had been the culprit. However, they did ascertain that the window had been smashed by a large rock.

I was damned no matter what I did. When I called the police for protection from him, he was not deterred in any way, shape, or form. Instead, just as soon as the coast was clear, he took immediate retaliation for my having spoiled his plans.

On the evening of October 26, I was stunned when the police showed up at my front door without my having called them first. I invited the officers inside, so they could question me about Chris's whereabouts.

"I have no idea. Why do you ask?"

"We had a call in from a certain Barrington Walker, who says that his vehicle was being chased by a car driven by your husband," the policeman informed me.

"That sounds like Chris, all right. But I haven't seen him stalking around here yet," I reported. "If you stick around long enough, he'll probably turn up eventually. You may as well save me a phone call and all the back and forth and wait for him here."

The officer, who I hadn't met before, chuckled. He was being polite, but it was clear he wasn't taking me seriously.

"Oh, one more thing," I called to them as they started out. "If he's not at home he may be at his girlfriend's house. Her name is Claire."

I scribbled her name and address on a piece of paper and handed it to him.

"Thank you ma'am," he said with a tip of the hat.

I went to the living room window and watched the officers head toward their car. At the same time, on the other side of the parking lot behind some bushes, I spotted Chris exiting his car. I had no idea what he planned to do, but I wasn't going to take any chances. While sliding open the window, I gestured madly and screamed out to the officers: "He's right over there! On the other side of those bushes!"

They heard me all right—but so did Chris. In the couple of seconds, the officers took to process my information and scout around for the right direction, Chris managed to escape back into his car and screech off. The officers leapt into their car, slammed the doors, flipped on the sirens, and went off in hot pursuit after the car zooming down the road with the headlights off.

A minute or so later, the skies darkened followed by a torrential downpour. I couldn't see a thing through the now closed window. I had a hunch that Chris's guardian angel— or was it guardian devil?—had come through for him yet again, causing the rainstorm that would enable him to make another successful getaway.

I had to wonder if such a thing as guardian angels exist in Judaism and, if so, where mine had ventured to and vanished. I made a mental note to ask my rabbi the next time I saw him.

Chapter Twelve

TIRE IRON
Jacksonville, FL: October 27, 1997
7:00 a.m.-12:30 p.m.

Nothing was going my way. I was jobless, drowning in debt, entrenched in legal fights, and unable to do anything to curb Chris's all-out assaults upon every aspect of my life.

Even my inner circle was dissipating, leaving me with few places to turn for emotional support outside of local friends. Things with Barrington remained the same—we had precious little time to focus on romance—to avoid adding more fuel to the raging Chris fire. My Mom grew so sick of hearing all of Chris's bellyaching on the phone that she suggested: "If he wants the kids, let him take them."

My answer was always: "I will never relinquish my children. Over my dead body will I walk away from my babies!"

Chris continued to influence the children at every opportunity. I tried to help reverse some of the damage inflicted upon Ashley by having her treated by a professional counselor, Tony Fiser, LCSW. After several sessions, Tony told Chris not to bother bringing her anymore because she was spending the entire forty-five minutes repeating what Chris had coached her to say. He saw right through what was going on but couldn't seem to do anything to break through it.

I was losing my grip on everything. I didn't think my life could get any worse, but, on October 27, it did.

***

Aside from all of the ongoing threats and other Chris-related nonsense, that Monday morning at the Hunters Way apartment complex started out like any other Fall day, except that Ashley had decided she wanted to spend the last couple of weeks with her father and, at Chris's urging, not see me at all. This gave me a queasy feeling, given all his influence over her and that he had been relentlessly working on turning her against me. Even Chris's mom warned him to never try and turn a child against a parent, as she will end up hating you instead. But he didn't listen to anyone. Since there weren't any specific court restrictions prohibiting her from temporarily living with him, I felt powerless to stop it.

The sky was a bit overcast and rainy, but otherwise it felt temperate and comfortable for this time of year in Jacksonville and sandals continued to be the primary footwear. My family and I set about our usual routines: Alese and Nick chattered incessantly as they brushed their teeth, combed their hair, and dressed. Alese picked out a sparkly pink and purple combination. She loved to dress in bright, frilly clothes. Nick, meanwhile, would have been happy wearing his superhero pajamas to school, but knew better than that and pulled on jeans and a polo shirt.

Once I was showered and clothed in a lightweight blue denim dress, I followed Seau, who barked at me all the way to the kitchen. I poured some food into his bowl and stroked his back as he crunched on the bits.

While downing my morning coffee, I thought about job opportunities and how I might receive specialized training in medical transcription. Clearly, my family wasn't going to last long on unemployment checks.

I prepared lunch for Alese and Nick, smearing peanut butter and jelly on slices of bread and smushing them together. I added a cheese stick, crisp apple slices, and a juice box into each respective lunchbox, along with the sandwiches.

After the kids ate some oatmeal, I ushered them out of the kitchen. Realizing it was already 8:30 a.m. I ordered, "Let's go guys."

The kids grabbed their lunchboxes and slung on their backpacks. Before heading toward the front door, I grabbed pepper spray off the table. I now did this every day out of habit, just in case Chris unexpectedly showed up. Ever since he started in with the death threats, I felt I needed to be prepared with some sort of protection.

The three of us made our way out of the apartment and down the second-floor stairway. The rain was spraying on us, but it wasn't heavy enough to warrant going back inside to fetch umbrellas. On the ground floor, we walked toward my Dodge Neon, so I could drive them to the Solomon Schechter Jewish Day School a few blocks away.

As I reached the vehicle and opened the passenger side to let the kids in, I glanced up and spotted *him* coming into view. I'd seen Chris in dozens of moods and crazy frames of mind, but never anything like this. Dressed like he was about to play softball in gray shorts, black hoodie, white athletic socks, and sneakers, he charged towards us from the heavily treed area behind the apartment building. He carried a gun by his stomach, positioned in such a way to ensure that I could see it. His eyes were laser-focused like a hit man or sniper, while his mouth was maniacally twisted.

I tried to process what was happening and jolt myself out of my state of disbelief. The scene was a total paradox, unfolding in slow motion yet sped up at the same time. My heart pounded. My brained filled with pins and needles. I was an unwilling actor in my own film.

He is coming at us with a gun.

My mind raced to only one thing: How was I going to protect my children?

He is going to murder my babies.

I froze. This was too much for me to bear. Before I knew it he was upon me, unleashing more rage than I ever thought possible—even for him. He bashed me to the ground with a blow to the head. My knees became scratched and bruised as I struck the pavement. I screamed as he barraged me with punches on my back, head, and neck.

"I have a knife!" he shouted. "Get in the car!"

A knife, too? Isn't the gun enough?

I was beaten and petrified but refused to go down without a fight. I wasn't about to freeze up again. I recalled something I learned from a self-defense course I'd attended a couple of years earlier.

Never allow someone to take you to another location away from help.

I had to do everything in my power to resist getting into the car with him. I struggled against his muscular frame, withstanding more blows and bracing myself for him to pull the trigger on the gun or stab me with the knife at any moment.

The pepper spray! If only I could get my hands on it...

I wrestled my hands free enough to grab the pepper spray, wrench it behind my back, and aim it in his direction. I sprayed randomly, determined not to let go until the vessel was emptied of its contents. I thought I'd hit him in the face—at least a little—but I couldn't be sure, as I was still turned away from him.

The knife fell out of his pocket as he heaved with frustration while hoisting me up and dumping me in the passenger seat. He crammed inside next to me and turned on the ignition.

This was just the beginning of my journey into hell.

***

"Look out—the kids!" I screamed.

Chris had put the car in reverse, and we were screeching backwards. Amidst all the commotion, I couldn't place where our children were positioned. Last I remembered, they were somewhere behind the car.

"They're fine, they left," he responded.

I craned my head back to peer through the rear window and confirmed that this was true: The kids were not in sight. I hoped they had fled to the apartment of our neighbors, Ana and her family, where they would be safe. I certainly didn't regard them as "fine" just because Chris hadn't hit them.

Later I learned that Ruby, Ana's teenage daughter, had witnessed the commotion and fight from her apartment. She flung open the living room window and screamed at the kids not to listen to Chris and instead come to her. She repeated the request a few times until they finally obeyed her.

Meanwhile, Chris shifted gear, reached across my body to turn the wheel, and drove forward. While the car was in motion and heading out of the parking lot into the road, he climbed over me into the driver's seat.

As he settled in and concentrated on driving, I conspired to make things as difficult as possible for him. I buckled my seat belt and then grabbed and jerked the steering wheel to crash the car.

Chris was always in good shape, and I was no match for him—even while he was driving. He flicked my hands away from the wheel. "You are not cooperating, Monique," he cautioned, elbowing me sharply in the jaw. "That's for Ashley."

As the tears rolled down my cheeks and my jaw throbbed, he said, "All I want to do is talk to you."

Talk to me? Is that all he wants? Is that why he beat me, flashed a gun and a knife at me, and tossed me into the car like one of the kids' backpacks? All because he just wants a conversation?

Now that the car was quiet, I had time to measure the massive swelling in my jaw and process the morning's events. The trauma of the experience no longer seemed like a film reel; it was my reality. This horror show was happening to me.

I visualized my abandoned children and started to cry. I felt my cheeks inflame and realized that my contact with Chris had caused pepper spray to transfer from him into my hair, which was rolling onto my face and mixing with my tears.

I was consoled by the fact that the pepper spray had fully kicked in and was causing greater discomfort to him than me. At least some of it had landed in his eyes, as they were tearing up and he was having difficulty seeing the road through the blur. He tried rubbing them, which only irritated them more. "Bitch," he growled.

His limited eyesight didn't deter him from intentionally driving like a lunatic. He sped through a grocery store parking lot and into an intersection, plowing straight through lights and traffic. When making a sharp turn around a corner, the bottom of the car smashed into a curb and dragged. Sparks flew by from the passenger side as we rode the rim down San Jose Blvd. onto a small service road behind a Taco Bell.

While Chris pulled over to change one of the tires, torrential rain started to come down. The windows became fogged from the moisture and my panicked breathing.

After turning off the car engine, he produced a roll of duct tape that had been concealed somewhere on his body and tore off a piece with his teeth. It became clear to me that he had planned for some, if not all, of this.

"Please don't do that," I protested. "I won't be able to breathe."

Chris knew from our years together that I had something of an issue with breathing through my nose. Shockingly, for the moment, at least, he still seemed to care about my well-being.

"Okay, I won't," he conceded. "But you better be quiet while I change the tire. I just need a little cooperation. All I want to do is talk with you."

I nodded to indicate that I intended "to cooperate." He stretched out the duct tape, wrapping it around both of my wrists several times and fastening them to the center gearshift.

He stepped outside in the rain to tend to the flat tire. I watched him circle to my side of the car with a tire iron when someone pulled up beside us in a black pickup truck. From the driver's seat, the man called out to Chris through his passenger window and across our car.

Tightening his grip on the tire iron, he shot a glance at me: *Do not say a word or else.* I had no doubt he would kill me—and possibly the Samaritan in the truck—if I were to scream out.

"Need any help?"

"Nope, we're all good."

As Chris spoke, I angled my head, so the truck driver would make eye contact with me and read my predicament without my having to say anything. I wasn't sure what he could discern on my face from such a distance—and through the rain, no less. But I had to try.

"Are you sure?" the truck driver asked.

"Yup, all good. Thanks."

The two exchanged waves before rolling up their windows. The truck driver moved on, not having noticed anything out of the ordinary.

Chris became drenched as he installed the spare tire. He was handy with all kinds of machinery from his years working on helicopters—as well as on our own cars—and was able to put the spare on in record time. In his rush, however, he left the tools lying behind a building. He returned to the car, sliding his hands through his soaked hair and mopping his face with a towel. He untied the tape, freeing my hands before starting the car and resuming his drive.

About twenty seconds later, the engine light flashed on the dashboard.

"What's wrong with your car?" he accused me, as if all the damage he'd just caused had been my fault.

"I don't know," I replied, not wanting to get into the blame game with him.

He continued to drive, ignoring the engine light. Every so often he broke the silence between us by blurting: "Remember, I just want to talk to you."

The more he said it, the more I hoped it was true. I wondered if he was taking us to a specific, pre-planned destination or just driving aimlessly, waiting for an idea to spontaneously present itself. Either way, the last place I wanted to be was in a broken-down car with this madman. I had to bide my time until I could escape, or he would come to his senses and let me go. The latter seemed like a far-fetched possibility, but I still held out hope.

Chris turned right on Loretta Road—a street lined with beautiful, spacious homes—when the car conked out in front of a particularly magnificent house. He flicked and twisted the ignition and stepped on the gas with increased frustration. The motor gagged and choked as if to beg, "Enough already!"

He yanked out the keys and slammed his palm on the steering wheel. He stepped out of the car and popped the hood. While he busied himself behind it, I looked around for any signs of life in this affluent area: residents, a cop, a postal worker—*anyone*. But the area seemed deserted.

The rain dissipated, and the clouds parted, allowing a ray of unexpected sunlight to poke through. The warmth and thick humidity spread into the car right away, and I had an impulse to find a way to open the door or window to let in some fresh air.

The change in weather was a reminder that I was in Florida—far away from my Mom, my childhood home, and my roots on the other end of the country. How I wished I could magically convert my hulking Dad into a caring and protective father who would suddenly appear, beat Chris to a pulp, and envelop me in a warm bear hug. All I wanted at that moment—and throughout the day—was to return to my children.

At any minute I expected to hear sirens flying by in pursuit of us. I imagined police surrounding the car with guns drawn, demanding Chris to let me go. There would be an ambush; I would be freed, unharmed.

Chris scrambled back-and-forth between the hood and the driver's seat, each time wrenching the keys in the ignition and flooring the gas pedal. He'd probably flooded it, but there was no mistaking the engine was dead anyway, and there was nothing he could do about it. After the fifth or sixth effort, he slammed the hood down and returned to the car. "I bet it's the oil since the oil light is on," he concluded. "When was the last time you had an oil change?"

Again it was my fault. My mind was swimming. I'd only recently purchased the car, so the idea of having to do an oil change hadn't even registered yet. "Never. I've never done one."

"Jesus, well, that explains it," he declared.

We remained parked on that street for about an hour. The whole day was slipping away. Chris didn't seem to have any intention of ever releasing me.

What are we doing here? He insists that he wants to do is "talk to me." Right. I wish I could believe that.

"We should find a phone, so I can call Beth Shorstein and ask her to get the kids," I said, referring to one of my closest friends. I knew she would do whatever she could to gather the kids and keep them safe.

"We need to go and buy oil for the engine," he stated.

"Aren't you worried about their safety?" I continued, playing to the one subject where I knew I could reach him. I could say a lot of negative things about Chris, but the one constant was his love of the kids, even if his view of healthy parenting was skewed.

"Please," I urged him. "Let me find a pay phone. The Department of Children and Families will have no choice but to take the kids away. The police will separate them from us and take them to foster care because they didn't go to school, and we're both missing."

After a few more seconds of hesitation, he arrived at a decision: "Come on, let's go. We're going to get oil for the car. But don't try anything—we're only here to talk."

I felt some room for optimism as we exited the car. Not only could I breathe and walk around without feeling like a prisoner, I thought I might be able to find an opening to make an escape and get to my children.

We walked a few blocks and entered a gas station. While we were at the register to ring up the container of engine oil, I spotted a pay phone. "Can I make a call?" I asked.

He looked at me as if to say, *What do you think I am, an idiot?*

"Wait until I'm done," he said.

After the purchase was completed, he escorted me to the telephone. He hovered over me as I lifted the receiver to my ear. I pressed the button up and down several times but didn't hear a dial tone.

"Don't bother with that," the cashier called out. "It don't work."

I hung up and looked Chris in the eye. "We need to find another phone. We have to be sure that someone other than the police or DCF has the kids."

"Fine," he agreed.

We continued further down the block toward a Winn-Dixie supermarket, which we both presumed would have at least one operational pay phone. We went through the parking lot past several parked cars and abandoned shopping carts. A couple of vehicles came and went in nearby aisles, but they were too far away from us for me to attempt to reach out to them.

We stepped through the automatic door to enter the supermarket. Familiar aromas filled my nostrils: fruits, vegetables, deli meats. It felt odd seeing so many people—male and female shoppers with carts, cashiers, and stock boys—all going about their normal business. To them it was just another regular Monday morning. By intent, Chris blocked them all from my view and shadowed around me, so I couldn't get anyone's attention.

We simultaneously noticed the telephones, which were in an open area to the side of the entranceway diagonal from the cash registers. We went straight to them. The supermarket was noisy with the usual chatter and occasional loudspeaker announcements, but I wondered if a phone conversation could be overheard if someone happened to be close enough and paying attention.

I was pleased to hear a dial tone the second I picked up a receiver. "Do you have any change?" I asked Chris.

He fumbled in his shorts pocket and handed me a couple of quarters, which I inserted into the phone.

"Don't forget," he reminded me. "You'll be home soon. I just want to talk to you."

What the hell? Hadn't we been talking? What's left to talk about?

I dialed my friend's phone number. As the phone started to ring, Chris tilted the phone to his ear, so he could listen in with me. It rang a couple more times before I heard Beth's familiar voice.

"Hi Beth, it's Monique."

"Monique! Where are you? Are you all right?"

"I need you to get my kids—all three of them."

"I already have all of them—they're fine. We're under police protection."

I became overwhelmed by thoughts and emotions. First, I experienced immense relief that my children were safe. I reconstructed the most likely scenario: During the attack on me, Alese and Nick scurried to my neighbor, who called the police and contacted Beth. She snapped into action by getting Ashley from Chris's apartment—since he had decided to allow her to stay home from school that day—and then picked up Alese and Nick, bringing them all back to her house.

Next I envisioned the fear my two kids were experiencing having seen their father terrorize me. Their lives had exploded around them with mommy and daddy fighting and then recklessly driving off somewhere for hours without any word. Now they were surrounded by a worried friend and armed police officers. Were they thinking Chris might show up there with a weapon and harm them?

I pictured my kids huddled at Beth's while she tried her best to reassure them. My eyes moistened as I searched for something to say that might ease their worries.

"I'll be home soon," I assured her, imagining the police officers eavesdropping and trying to find any clues to target our location.

"Monique, tell me where you are!"

Chris's eyes fastened on me, communicating: *Don't do something stupid.*

I had no choice except to repeat the party line: "Chris just wants to talk to me. It's okay."

He shot a look indicating the call was over, and it was time to leave. "I have to go. I'll see you soon."

I hung up. I peered around, wondering if any of the employees and customers had detected anything out of the norm in our behavior. No one said or did anything, so I presumed this wasn't the case.

"Let's go," he prompted.

My window of opportunity to scream out and get help was dwindling. As he directed me out of the store, all I could think about was how I longed for things to return to normal for the kids and me that afternoon.

Ashley has swim practice. Alese has dance class. Nick has tee-ball practice.

We trudged back to the car. My hopes of being rescued were dashed.

Now that the kids were safe, I needed to come up with some way to convince him to turn himself in. This had already gone too far.

We returned to the secluded area where we'd left the car. No one was in the vicinity. "Get back in," he ordered.

I followed his orders and watched him resume work, putting the oil he'd just purchased to use. He flopped back in the car and wiped his grimy hands off with a towel.

"Aren't you going to see if the car starts?"

"It's time for our talk," he said.

Okay, fine, whatever. Let's just get this talk over with so I can the hell out of here.

"What went wrong with our marriage, Monique? We were pretty good together, weren't we?"

"We've been miserable for years, and you know it."

"We've had our share of blow-ups...but don't a lot of couples go through that?"

Sure. Those in hostile relationships.

"I just want to live in peace and the kids to have a peaceful home."

His expression seemed to have softened a bit. I wondered if I was getting through to him. "Things will be okay, Chris.

If you turn yourself in, you can do some time and move on with your life."

"I will not go to jail," he snarled.

"Don't you see how bad all this is? Think about what it's doing to the kids. Think about your parents. You'll eventually get caught and arrested. Your parents' house is on the line. All they've worked for is attached to your bond. Do you really want to do that to them?"

"I want you to take care of the kids, since I won't be around."

"What do you mean?"

"Like I said, I will not go to jail."

I wondered if he meant that he planned to flee to avoid jail time or do something more drastic, such as suicide. If it was the latter, at least it didn't sound like he planned to take me with him, since he expressed his desire to have me care for the children in his absence.

Whatever the case, it concluded our "big talk"—at least for the time being. He inserted the key in the ignition and turned it. To my surprise, it started right up. He reacted as if he knew it would work all along.

As we pulled out of the spot, I wondered if he planned to drop me off and then take my car somewhere to go on the lam or find a spot to end it all. Either way, I held out renewed hope that I might make it through this day without further incident and injury.

But the car wobbled and sputtered a mere couple of blocks until we entered a development of single-family homes under construction. We coasted into a subdivision when the engine light flashed on again. No one was around— not even the builders working on the new constructions.

We entered a wet paved road, passed a model house, turned a corner, and pulled in front of a newly completed residence: white with stucco, big windows without shutters, and an attached two-car garage. A curved cement walkway led to the front door.

Once we were parked, he turned off the engine. It was unclear if this had been his intended destination all along, if he was just giving up on the car, if he had an impulse to resume "our talk," or a combination of all three.

"What do you see in Barrington?"

"For starters, he's nice and kind."

"I can be, too. Don't you see how good I am with the children?"

"At times—and that's with *them*. What about with me? You've always been very critical and judgmental of me. And you've physically harmed me several times—including today. You also have been losing your temper more with the kids, and it's unnecessary."

"I'm sorry about that," he tried to soothe me as he crowded in closer. He caressed my hair and added, "This will be my last chance to be with you."

Dear God, no. Anything but this.

"No, please—*don't*," I declined. "I don't want to."

He shifted over to me on the passenger seat. Despite my emphatic protest, his hands snaked around me.

"I said 'no,' Chris. *I mean it.*"

He pawed and probed until I felt his fingers raise my blue jean dress. With one tug he ripped off my underwear and flung the garment aside.

"Stop…stop!"

A moment later he pounced on my body and entered me.

"Please…stop…"

I turned away as he repeatedly thrust himself into me while groaning and grunting in my ear. I tried to tune him out and put myself somewhere else, but it was impossible: The seat and his body weight on me were so uncomfortable and his sweat, sounds, and odor made my flesh crawl.

I prayed he would just complete his business and let me get back to my children.

Chapter Thirteen

GARDEN TOOL
Jacksonville, FL: October 27, 1997
12:30 p.m.-2:00 p.m.

Mercifully, he was done in less than sixty seconds. Breathing heavily, he climbed back to the driver's seat.

I felt humiliated and filthy as I sank down in the seat. I longed for a shower to remove every trace of him from me.

Thank God I had my tubes tied back in Japan. But why did I have to have my period now? It's making this dreadful experience more repulsive—not that he seems to care about my condition one way or the other.

For what it was worth, I now assumed he'd had a change of heart. He'd done his worst and my ordeal might soon come to an end. He took what he wanted—this was his endgame all along, wasn't it?—and now it was time to move on. His next statement helped further this belief for me.

He seemed matter-of-fact and chipper as he suggested, "I'm going to go and see if there's anyone in that house who can help us with the car."

"Okay."

This time he didn't seem to feel the need to issue any kind of warning to me as he stepped out of the car and left me by myself. Why should he worry? He was confident in his assumption that he'd stripped me of any fight I might have had left. To at least some extent, he was right. I was desperate and afraid and didn't want to risk setting him off.

I watched him through the window as he strolled across the walkway toward the empty house. I was distracted when I felt several weird objects underneath me: pieces of plastic that hadn't been in my car before Chris had shown up. I held one up and stared at it. The realization of what they were sent me right back inside a suspense movie.

Industrial strength one-way zip ties, the kind that need to be cut in order to be removed. First the gun, then the knife, next the duct tape...now these zip ties falling out of his pocket. It dawned on me that this had been premeditated. He planned from the get-go to bag me up and throw me out in a trash bag after having raped and murdered me.

I—the naïve heroine—had unknowingly been in the presence of a sociopathic killer right from the opening scene.

While Chris was still somewhere by the house with his back turned to me, I collected all the zip ties, opened the car door a crack, slipped them through, and dropped them in rolling rainwater alongside the curb. My eyes followed them on their journey as the water pressure carried them a safe distance down the storm drain. I gently pulled the car door closed.

My body flinched when he rocketed back into the driver's seat. "There's no one around who can help us," he reported.

I couldn't determine how hard he had been searching for assistance and whether he even cared. While meandering by the house, he might have been assessing the situation and plotting his next move. Perhaps it sank in that he had already gone past the point of no return with all the crimes he'd already committed: assault, kidnapping, and reckless endangerment. Now he could add rape to the list. What difference did it matter to him what he did next? The outcome would be the same—if he were to get caught. I remained convinced he had not done anything that couldn't somehow be sorted out if he were to come clean to the police.

He started up again with more idle chatter about our marriage, our kids, and our life together. He wanted it all to work. He loved our kids—so he said.

Yeah, whatever.

He droned on for several minutes until he asked, "The sex was always good with us, wasn't it?"

How am I supposed to answer that after he'd just forced himself on me against my consent? Is he delusional enough to think I can look past that and conjure up a pleasurable intimate moment with him? Does he think that a reminder of the good ole' days might make me want him again?

But I didn't dare risk saying something he didn't want to hear. I doubted his narcissistic ego could take it.

I turned away from him to look through the window while pretending I was someone—and somewhere—else. I bit my lip and compelled an "Mn-hmn." I hoped my response had been good enough for him to change the subject.

After a slight hesitation, I heard him open the door and head out.

What now?

I watched him circle behind the car to my passenger door, which he tugged open. He grabbed me by the neck and arm, wrenching me from my seat. While maintaining his locked grip on me, he opened the back door and tossed me on my back into the cushion.

He stood above me while fumbling in his shorts. "You should enjoy this," he leered. "It's going to be my last time."

Oh God...no. Not again. Couldn't he just kill himself and skip doing this to me?

"Please...Chris...*no...don't!*"

My pleas were for naught. The previous time hadn't been enough for him. Maybe it went by too rushed and was uncomfortable for him in the front seat. Who knows? Once again, he pounced on top and inside of me—heaving, panting, and braying like a barnyard animal. My body quaked in torment.

Pulling up his shorts, he sat up and wiped his forehead.

He granted me enough room to adjust myself and sit up. The car even felt more claustrophobic and sticky than before.

He broke the silence by uttering: "You must really hate me."

Ding-ding! What perception. Such genius.

"Please…stop doing all of this," I implored. I continued to delude myself into thinking it was possible to reason with him. "What's the point of it? I don't want to be doing this with you."

"You must really hate me," he repeated.

Yes. I do. More than anyone else on the planet.

"I just want to get home to the kids," I whispered, knowing I was wasting my breath.

He droned on with the same old tropes while we lingered in the backseat. "Your relationship with this Barrington guy is completely inappropriate…."

Inappropriate! Does he hear himself?

"…Ashley tells me that she, Alese, and Nick see you in bed with him all the time."

Never. Not once. But what's the point of arguing? He is never going to be convinced of anything other than what's already in his sick, twisted brain.

The minutes went by at a snail's pace. I wondered if he was biding time to reclaim enough energy for a third go-round against my will. During a lull in his accusation-filled monologue, I was able to find a wedge. I spoke in the most sympathetic tone I could muster: "Chris, I need to get home—right now. Think about the kids. They're scared. They're worried about me—about *us*…. Let me go with you to turn yourself in. We can head back to the Winn-Dixie and make a simple phone call. We can end all of this peacefully."

To my astonishment, he relented: "Okay, I'm ready to go."

Had I really gotten through to him? It seemed far

too good to be true. My hopes were raised for a fleeting moment—until the other shoe dropped.

"Let's go look at that house first."

"Why?" I asked.

He refused to answer as he opened the door on my side, gesturing for me to leave. Desperate to try anything that might expedite his surrender, I adjusted my blue denim dress. I considered putting my undies back on, but they were too torn and disheveled to try. I slid out of the car and advanced toward the house. When he joined me at the curb, I looked around for someone—*anyone*—but not a single person was in sight. I also noticed that it was again starting to rain, despite the partial sunshine.

I again tried to prod answers out of Chris as he passed by. "Why do you want to look at that house? Do you think there's a phone inside? Are you interested in buying it?"

"I just want to see what's in there," he replied.

I trailed after him, noticing the recently planted sod lawn and shrubs accompanied by the scent of moist cedar mulch. "How will we even get in there? Isn't it locked?"

He didn't answer, but at the least seemed calm and agreeable. In denial about the plastic ties, I clung to the possibility that he was preparing to turn himself in.

He swiveled the front doorknob. I thought for sure he'd find it locked, but it easily opened. It occurred to me he discovered it was unlocked when he had approached it earlier; I was too preoccupied discarding the ties at the time to notice what he had been doing.

If that had been the case, however, why hadn't he entered the house and searched for a phone when he had the chance? Why had he withheld that information from me? Most likely, I figured, he found it unlocked and then returned to the car to bide time until after he'd violated me for the second time. He must have changed his mind, realizing his appetite hadn't been fully gratified.

I searched for clues in his face and body language as he

made his way into the house. I couldn't determine anything specific one way or the other. He motioned for me to accompany him. I kept a distance between us but walked in his direction, thinking that there wasn't much left for him to do that he hadn't already inflicted upon me.

I inhaled the familiar odor of newly installed carpeting and fresh paint. The new stucco home was vacant—completely devoid of any trace of inhabitants. There was no furniture or décor to speak of. The walls were stark white and freakishly clean. There weren't even electrical wires or cables hanging from the walls or exposed holes anywhere. It was picture perfect, ready for real estate agents and buyers to parade through and conduct their walk-throughs.

Something about this made me uneasy, hesitant. The realization that there was no chance in a billion we were going to find a telephone in this house became abundantly clear.

Why, then, are we here? What is he doing? What is he thinking? Whatever it is, let's just get it over with, so I can get to the kids.

I'm cooperating...

I'm not making any smart remarks...

If I just continue like this, it'll all be over soon...

Inexplicably, he rounded a slight bend and slinked through an opening into what I presumed was the garage. I followed a few feet behind him and breathed a sigh of relief as I caught a glimpse of outdoor daylight. This signaled that not only had he entered the garage, but the door leading outside was open, and I had a place through which to exit.

"You can come this way and get out over here," he called as his bending forefinger teased the words *C'mere, it's okay.*

I stepped into the garage. Like the interior of the house, it appeared spotless and smelled brand new. In the center was a desk, probably upon which the construction workers had laid out unfurled paper building plans for review. To the side were several ordinary garden tools leaning against the wall. Chris went straight toward them, specifically selecting a rectangular digging shovel with two points at the end and moving it away from the others.

"W-w-why did you take that?" I asked, panic rising in my throat.

"I just wanted to see what they had here," he answered.

I felt like an animal ensnared in a trap. My fight or flight instinct went out of whack, sensing something horrific was imminent—far worse than anything else that had transpired until that point.

I made a run for it. Escape was the only thing on my mind.

I heard him bolt after me and close the gap. I sensed his presence looming from behind and crooked my head back to get a look. His hand covered my mouth. I reacted by chomping on his finger. He retaliated by biting me on the left upper arm. He slammed my head straight down to the concrete garage floor. I lay on the ground in a daze.

Out of the corner of my half-opened eye I saw him reach for the shovel and rotate it over his shoulder like a baseball bat to land a blow. I knew it was coming at me lightning-fast but did not have the wherewithal in my condition to fight back or even know which part of me to protect. There was no time to think or speak. The metal end thundered against the back of my skull. I was vaguely aware of my own blood spattering past my face. My hands oozed with gobs of blood. I became numb and disoriented as the reverberation sent shockwaves from head to toe and back up again.

He didn't waste any time dragging me on the ground by the top of my dress. My legs scraped the ground as he hauled me out of the garage and several feet into the driveway. He slung me over his shoulder like a ragdoll in one arm while holding the shovel aloft in the other.

I didn't believe I was capable of speech, but somehow the words managed to come out: "Please...don't! The kids... think of the kids!"

I bobbed up and down—helpless as he carried me across the street. With my head dropping, I could see the trail of blood from my skull blotting the ground.

Before I knew it, we were no longer out in the open. I was looking down at brush, leaves, and twigs. The world began to seal up around me as we went past a morass of thick bushes and trees. Flashes of mist and faint daylight sparkled through the tree branches in the form of kaleidoscopic dots.

I am in the woods. He has brought me here to finish me off and bury me.

We kept moving forward...I couldn't possibly know where we were headed. I didn't think even he knew, except that he probably figured it had to be deep enough in the woods to avoid being seen or heard.

He tossed me to the ground face down. Either he was growing tired or decided we were concealed enough. I prayed I could make one last attempt to reason with him and beg for mercy.

But he didn't give me the chance. As I lay whimpering on a pile of dead, wet leaves on my left side, he reared back and struck me several more times on the back of my head with the shovel. I instinctively blocked my head with my hands; my fingers and knuckles were on the receiving end of most of the pounding. My large garnet ring—a birthstone, a gift to myself for having quit this miserable marriage—smashed through my skin to the bone.

He paused as I slumped down on the ground—motionless. I lay as still as I possibly could.

My only option is to play dead. Do not so much as twitch. Do not breathe.

He pried open my right eye and felt the pulse on my neck. Meanwhile, my pulse echoed like a bass drum in my head.

Is this going to give me away?

I continued to remain still and struggle to halt my breathing. But my efforts weren't nearly enough to convince him.

"You're not dead yet," he concluded.

He stomped his foot on my hands and crunched them to the ground. He shoved my broken fingers out of the way, pinning them down so he could land clean shots.

He pummeled me several more times with the shovel. Each blow echoed in my skull like a jackhammer hitting steel.

Everything was foggy. Fading to black.

I heard a voice trilling in the air. "Can you hear me?"

I didn't respond. Move. Or breathe. I concentrated solely on subduing my pulsating heart.

"Can you hear me?"

I do. But I'm playing dead.

He lifted my right leg and dragged my listless body several feet deeper into the woods. I remained lifeless, prostrate.

Stay still...your life depends on it.

A hush spread throughout the woods. I could feel his presence nearby. Watching me. Studying me. Making sure the deed was successfully executed.

I thought I heard him shifting away and perhaps the sound of the shovel being discarded. Footsteps fading through the woods.

Do not move. This could be a trick. A test. He could be lurking out there somewhere, waiting to strike again.

I just lay there…and lay there…and lay there…

I drifted into unconsciousness, waking only when flies and other insects landed on me, waiting for my flesh to decay, so they could start their feast. The rain resumed in full force, cascading on me like any other inanimate object.

I began to feel uncontrollable shivers and shakes. I knew these were the fatal prelude of going into shock.

Soon I was going to be dead for real.

Chapter Fourteen

SLIVER OF SIGHT
Jacksonville, FL: October 27, 1997
2:00 p.m.-7:00 p.m.

Is he gone? Maybe...but how can I possibly be sure?

I don't know exactly how long I lay there. I lost all sense of time. Everything was spinning in my head. My lifeblood was pouring out of me. Each passing second I remained frozen in place brought me that much closer to my grave.

No. I am not ready to die. And I will not let that murderous bastard win.

I have to take the risk. I can't hang on much longer. We could be somewhere near a body of water, which means alligators might be lurking around. This is Florida, after all...

I must find help. It's now or never. The only thing I can do is to find a way to get up—or at least stand enough to move forward and head out of the woods. My only option is to reach the street and hope to God someone will be there and see me.

But what if no one is around? We spent a good portion of the day in a neighborhood with homes under construction where none of the workers ever appeared.

Worse, what if HE turns up again? There is no way I can survive another attack.

First, I had to lift my pounding head—which was unable to move a fraction left or right—and see what I could in the surrounding area. My eyes, which I imagined looked like mini plums, were nearly swollen shut except for tiny slits that allowed slivers of sight to poke through. I had no peripheral vision whatsoever. Through my blood caked eyebrows, I peered outward and swore I spotted a narrow clearing out of the woods.

I can't believe it. My contact lenses are actually still in my eyes—and I can see I am not that far from the street...

Trying to focus in the direction of the passage out of the woods, I made out a brown, work-style station wagon parked by the curb. In the driver's seat sat a black middle-aged man—a construction worker, perhaps.

My head drooped down.

This can't be possible. I'm hallucinating. The street had been so desolate...

I raised my head up again to confirm what I thought I'd seen. The man was still in the car, now sipping coffee from a Styrofoam cup.

He's real. I must reach him. I don't have the strength to scream out. Time is ticking. He's my only chance. I pray he's not gone by the time I get there—IF I can get anywhere near him.

I attempted to force my body up with my hands and arms. Big mistake. They were utterly useless. The throbbing from the myriad breaks and bruises was unbearable.

I had to concentrate on using the areas of my body that were at least somewhat functioning and responsive. I wailed as I grappled with heaving my torso using just my hips and abdomen. Once the top of my body was at a forty-five-degree angle, I took a deep breath and applied some pressure on my legs. I proceeded with caution, unsure if I was at all capable of sustaining my own weight and balancing myself on my feet. I didn't think I would have a second chance if I were to fail with my head hitting the ground.

Slow and easy...

Miraculously, I was able to rise—sort of. I hunched forward and sideways, incapable of standing erect. I staggered forward.

Oh my God. He could be anywhere and come at me again. He could tackle me from behind, and I won't be able to do a single thing to defend myself.

Petrified, I stumbled onward. My bones, muscles, and joints felt like they were at war with each other. A few were up to the challenge of motion; many were not. My limbs dangled as I hobbled, zombie-like, one half step at a time. It felt like the clearing was miles away. Still, I kept going.

Watch out for the tree branch…and that bush. If only I could see better…

At last, I hobbled through the opening and into the street.

I made it!

I collapsed to the ground. I heard footsteps approaching but couldn't lift my head to see who was there.

"Don't move," he cautioned. "I will get you help and be right back."

As he shifted away, I begged him: "Please….don't go… don't leave me…"

Once again I mustered enough strength to get up on my feet. The man hovered nearby, unsure of what to do as my limp body swayed towards the passenger door of his car. He opened the door, and I flopped inside.

"Please…don't leave me."

"I'm just going to drive you to that model home over there. There are people inside—they will get help," he assured me.

He hopped into the driver's seat and floored it down the block until we reached the model home he had referenced. "I'm just going inside there—I'll be right back," he said, heading out of the car.

As he scurried off and disappeared from my view I murmured, "No…"

A few moments later, he returned from the house with a concerned man and woman.

"Don't worry," my savior comforted me. "An ambulance is on the way."

Hold on just a little bit longer. You can do it. You've made it this far...

My tortured eyes snapped shut.

***

"What is your name?"

"Who did this to you?"

"Do you have anyone we can contact?"

I did my best to answer questions—first from the strangers who summoned help and then from the two EMTs from Jacksonville Fire and Rescue who assessed my frightful condition on arrival. At this stage I didn't even bother to try to open my eyes. I was safe, at last, with some hope of survival in the hands of strangers—which was all that mattered.

"Female, thirty-one years of age, extensive wounds to her head reportedly inflicted by her husband with a garden shovel..."

"Patient is pale, weak..."

"I'm not reading a pulse..."

"Got it."

"BP not readable..."

"Multiple open wounds throughout the skull..."

"Severe swelling to both hands, presumed breaks and/or fractures to the digits..."

They set to work, first wrapping an Aspen Cervical Collar around my neck.

I don't know what hurts most—my head, my hands, or this stupid collar.

After three attempts, they were able to insert a needle in my arm for an IV.

"All right, Monique," a male EMT said. I could sense his presence up close to my face. "You'll be okay. We're doing our best to keep you stable. We are going to take you to the hospital by helicopter. It's the fastest way."

He waited until I registered this information with a blind nod.

"The Life Flight helicopter should be here any minute. Hang in there."

True to the EMT's word, shortly thereafter I heard a helicopter making its approach and landing nearby. I was raised onto a gurney and carried toward the craft. The EMTs lifted me up and secured me aboard the helicopter. Before I knew it, I was ascending. The choppy reverberations of the cycling propellers echoed in my ears. The sounds and vibrations were intolerable.

"Is that gray matter in her ears?"

"I don't know…"

I am going to die in this helicopter.

They flew me to the nearest trauma center, University Medical Center, Jacksonville. We couldn't have landed soon enough.

The nurses wheeled me into an elevator, down a corridor, and into the emergency trauma room, where I was swarmed by the medical team. It was such an odd feeling to be a patient in a trauma room when, not that long ago, I had been working on a trauma team. The room became a flurry of noisy medical activity around me with everyone talking at once and equipment being shuffled around.

"Monique," a deep male voice addressed me. "My name is Dr. Simon Lampard. I'm your attending trauma physician. I know you are in substantial pain—we'll give you medications for that. We have to run a bunch of tests to determine the extent of your injuries. Don't worry, we'll take good care of you."

"Thank you, doctor," I mumbled.

I felt him lightly touch a piece of my shoulder he knew was undamaged. He had successfully managed to provide some comfort and security for me, despite everything I was enduring. It took a long time for those painkillers to start kicking in, though, and even then, there was only so much they could do.

I heard Dr. Lampard command the room as I was poked and prodded all over my body. After a while, things settled down as I became stable and out of immediate life-threatening danger. A nurse whisked me down the hall and into a scanning room, where I was delicately adjusted onto my back onto an icy metal slab.

My head and legs fidgeted as I squirmed through the pain and discomfort.

"Stop moving," the female technician ordered. "You must lie completely still."

No matter how hard I tried, I could not do as she asked.

She grew increasingly frustrated with me: "*Stop moving.*"

"I can't," I groaned. "Just a pillow…please?"

"I'm sorry," she answered. "You can't move at all during the CT scan. I promise, after it's done, we'll do everything we can to help you get comfortable."

My head yearned for a soft place to rest. Anything between my head and the metal stone underneath would have been a gift.

The tests seemed endless; I was escorted from one room to the next.

Blood work. CT scans. X-rays.

Sometime later, I was moved to the ICU where I could rest my aching head on soft pillows. Warm blankets were layered over me.

If only they would take off this damn neck collar…

Dr. Lampard entered the room and stood bedside, from where he informed me of the extent of my injuries: "All right Monique," he began. "I'll give everything to you straight.

You have a basilar skull fracture…six-centimeter and eight-centimeter lacerations to your scalp…a series of fractures to your ulna…"

"Oh," I ruminated.

"You won't be surprised to hear you have numerous fractures to several fingers."

"My head?"

"As impossible as it may seem, considering the harshness of the blows, you are not only fortunate to still be alive, there is a reasonable chance that your brain will recover, and you won't have permanent damage. You are conscious and can speak and move, which are excellent signs. It's too early to tell for sure, however."

It was only later I discovered what drugs were pumped into me:

- 5000 units of heparin twice per day
- acetaminophen 650 mg. every six hours
- morphine 4 mg./IV every 4 hours
- diazepam 5 mg./IV every 6 hours
- Ancef 1 gm./IV every 8 hours
- promethazine 12.5 mg/IV for nausea every 6 hours

The barrage continued non-stop. Lab work. Dressing changes. Examinations from rotating specialists. Stitches sewn into my head. Braces attached to my arms and fingers. Then I heard the sound of a camera shutter working. Flash photographs of my injuries were being snapped.

"What…are you doing?" I asked.

"I'm sorry, I was trying not to disturb you," a male voice said. "I'm the evidence technician. I need to take pictures for the police crime file."

After my "photo shoot" was done, I was able to rest, and try in vain to clear my head of everything that had happened that day.

When will I see my children?

***

At around 6 p.m. that evening, I received a visit from Detective J.T. Royal of the Jacksonville Sheriff's Department. He had dark hair with a well-groomed beard and was impeccably dressed in a suit and tie. I described the day's events to him in gory detail, and how I had spent hours trying to convince Chris to turn himself in while believing he would eventually let me go. He stopped when he thought he had collected enough information for the time being and the questioning had become too overwhelming.

After the Detective departed a nurse informed me, "A rape team will be coming in to see you soon and take samples."

"Okay," I gulped.

This sounded just awful, but I knew it had to be done while there was evidence to be found and documented.

A woman from the Sexual Assault Treatment Center introduced herself as Ms. Murray before interviewing me and conducting a thorough examination.

"Everything will be explained before doing it," Ms. Murray reassured me. "We'll do our best to make it quick."

Despite Ms. Murray and her team's best efforts, there was no avoiding the fact that I was 100 percent exposed to total strangers. It was beyond humiliating.

My legs were spread. My pubic hair was combed. My legs were swabbed. Samples were taken from my vaginal area.

How much more of this will I have to endure?

Drifting in and out of sleep, I gazed through the glass window of my hospital room toward my door. I saw a man in police uniform leaning against the wall, just outside of my room. I should have felt safe that I had a guard and was protected, but I was flooded with anxiety. My mind insisted on replaying the day's events like a film loop.

Why had he done this to me? Where is he now?

My body jolted. I imagined that Chris was going to spring out from behind a curtain; sneak past the nurses' station; overpower the policeman outside my door; and strangle and suffocate me.

My eyes opened: The policeman outside my door had vanished.

I screamed out in terror—which wasn't all that disruptive, considering my condition—while desperately reaching for and grasping the call button. I pressed it with my fractured fingers to summon the nurse.

A nurse scrambled in: "What is it? Everything okay?"

"Where is the policeman? The one guarding my door?" I panicked.

"Don't worry," she dismissed. "He's still here, he just walked down the hall. He's not far."

"Will you please stay with me until he comes back?"

"I'll tell you what," she proposed. "I'll go and see where he went."

"Can I have something to drink—to sip? I'm so thirsty..."

"No, you can't have anything by mouth," she barked. "Don't you realize how injured you are?"

I thought she was coming at me a bit harsh. Since she knew I was raw from the day's trauma, why was she speaking to me this way?

"Until we confirm whether you need surgery or not, you cannot have anything," she added.

All right, Nurse Ratchet, whatever you say.

Once the officer returned to his post, I was able to relax and succumb to sleep. By the time I awoke, Detective Royal had returned and filled me in on what had become of his suspect.

Chapter Fifteen

STAKEOUT
Jacksonville, FL: October 27-November 7, 1997

While I was fighting for my life, being rescued, and treated at the hospital, Chris did everything he could to evade capture by the police.

The police went on a manhunt after him throughout the Mandarin area, and the media was notified. Officers questioned anyone who might know his whereabouts, including Claire, the woman he was dating. She informed them that she'd seen a story about the kidnapping on the 10 o'clock news and was scared. Not only didn't she know where Chris might be hiding, she was clueless about his criminal record and how he had been stalking me these past several months.

The police set up active surveillance and a stakeout at Chris's apartment complex into the wee hours of the night. They found Chris's "hidden" car—the gold Saturn—and punctured all four tires, so it could not be used to make a getaway. There was blood evidence inside, suggesting that at some point he had shown up and considered escaping in it.

Despite the wide net cast, Chris still managed to evade the policemen's watchful eyes for several hours and find his way back inside his residence. He left armed with a butcher knife and snuck outside, where police saturated the area.

At around 3 a.m. the following morning, an officer named Michael Perry spotted Chris walking in the vicinity. Originally, he wasn't on duty or supposed to be there, but the undersheriff summoned all hands on deck the moment I was kidnapped to do whatever was necessary to apprehend Chris.

Chris froze as the two locked eyes. Instead of surrendering, he rabbited into a six-foot culvert.

Officer Perry radioed his partner, Officer Slayton, who was on foot and near the location.

"The suspect saw me," he reported. "He ran into a small water tunnel. I think I have him trapped."

"Don't let him get away," came the voice on the other end. "I'll be right there."

Officer Perry extracted his .40-caliber Glock pistol from his holster and called out: "Police! Come out with your hands up!"

Chris meandered out of the culvert, but his hands were not raised. He was doing something peculiar with his hands.

"Get down on the ground!" the officer commanded. "Stop what you're doing! Put the knife down—*now*!"

Instead of obeying, Chris screamed something and charged at the officer with the upraised bloody knife. The officer fired at him…again…again…and again. Three shots pierced his body—one in the foot, one in the chest, and another in his lower ribs. He tried to get up but collapsed in front of the officer, the knife plunking down to the ground by his side.

Officer Slayton and Sergeant O'Neil cuffed him and read him his rights before calling an ambulance. He could now see that Chris had been slicing his wrists and even into his throat with the butcher knife, where lines of blood had formed.

Once again the Jacksonville Fire and Rescue arrived at the scene. They made sure he was stable for transport and then drove him to the hospital…

***

Early the following morning, Barrington visited me in my hospital room and, with bated breath, informed me of the latest news: "They found him. Chris has been shot by the police."

"Is he dead?" I hopefully asked.

Silence.

"Answer me: *Is he dead?*"

"No," Barrington lamented.

"Which hospital will he go to?"

Again, no answer.

"*What hospital is he going to?*" I repeated.

"He's already here," Barrington reported. "After surgery, if he survives, he'll be moved to this ICU."

Oh God. Why me? Even after everything I've gone through, he still has to haunt me.

***

The news of Chris being treated in the same hospital grated on me. However, as the day progressed, I was distracted by the comings and goings of several welcome visitors.

First I was awakened from a nap by the sound of people whispering in a corner of my room. I adjusted myself as much as possible until I recognized the warm, friendly faces: Dan Wilensky, along with other attorney friends I knew from the Jacksonville Jewish Center—Evan Yegelwel and Jeffery Morris. This astute legal trio was not only there to pay their respects and see how I was doing, they had also assembled to brainstorm legal maneuvers that would benefit and protect the kids and me.

Not long after, I was elated when Ashley arrived—the only child who was old enough to be allowed to visit me at the ICU at this point—accompanied by Beth, who assured me that Alese and Nick were fine.

Ashley sobbed, "Mom..."

I gave her the opportunity to cry it out for a few minutes prior to offering her comfort through my splinted hands. "It will be okay," I soothed, hoping to change the subject. I knew that, even in my time of need, it was crucial for things to remain as normal as possible for my children. "Remember to fix Nick's lunch and his snack.... Make sure Alese goes to ballet.... And don't forget to do your homework.... I love you."

I couldn't bear seeing Ashley so upset. I could only imagine what she was really thinking as she came to terms with the brutality of her father's actions. At the least, I felt certain that the spell of his brainwashing had at last been broken.

Other family members flocked in. My Mom and Uncle Rodney took the first flights they could catch to Jacksonville and rushed straight to the hospital. It felt so good to see them both and feel their unconditional warmth and support.

Unbeknownst to me, after seeing me in my wrecked condition, Rodney snuck off to find Chris in the hospital with the intent of finishing what the police had started. Security managed to intervene before my uncle could get to him and barred him from the hospital.

I was disappointed to hear that my Dad wasn't coming, especially since Jan, his second wife, told my Mom that he was devastated by the news of the attack. He decided he would fly in if I were to need him later, as he believed that the worst time for him to see me was when everyone else was there. This response confounded me.

A couple of days passed. As astonishing as it was that I pulled through without having sustained long-term brain damage, it was perhaps even more remarkable that Chris survived his near-fatal injuries. In fact, he was starting to receive his own share of out of town visitors, including his parents. The probability of the two family factions encountering in the elevator or in the ICU and clashing became a genuine cause for concern, especially after Uncle Rodney's behavior. The circus became complete with reporters trampling back and forth to get any kind of statement from Chris's family, my family, or the medical staff.

Less than a couple of days into my recuperation, my doctor appeared in my room with an announcement: "Monique, the hospital is not equipped to handle hostile relatives and bothersome media like this. I'm afraid one of you must leave. Since you're in better medical shape then he is, it should be you."

After everything I had endured, was it wise for me to be home without hospital supervision? Why should that rapist and attempted murderer get preferential treatment over *me*, the victim?

On the other hand, after my initial surprise to hear that I was in good enough shape to be discharged, I found myself longing to return home and be with my children. I was also happy to put some distance between Chris and me. I couldn't help but feel paranoid that, despite his critical condition and the armed guards outside his door and mine, he might find a way to attack me. I needed to put all of this behind me as soon as possible and get my life back on track. I didn't have a job or any money in my bank account though, thankfully, my medical expenses were covered under our Humana military insurance. I willingly accepted the doctor's offer to continue my recovery at home.

My Mom and Uncle Rodney were displeased by this decision, to say the least. To them I still looked like a train wreck survivor who was unable to do the most basic everyday functions on my own. I sympathized with their predicament. Not only didn't they believe I was ready to leave the hospital, they had to assume the burden of caring for me, since we couldn't afford a nurse. My medical condition required a great deal of oversight: managing my prescription intake; replacing my bandages; helping me eat and go to the bathroom; giving me regular sponge baths (which my uncle understandably refused to do); ensuring that the nasty Aspen collar remained on my neck at all times; and chauffeuring me to frequent appointments with neurologists, trauma departments, orthopedists, and numerous other miscellaneous medical professionals. Plus, my Mom and uncle had to navigate the schedules and needs of my children.

Despite the relentless emotional and physical pain and discomfort from my experience, I was elated about one overriding upside: I was going home to be with my children. Nothing else in the world mattered.

***

The sun glared in my eyes throughout the drive home. My heart raced as my Mom and Uncle Rodney assisted me into the house and settled me in bed. I eagerly waited for the kids to come home from school.

Several hours passed until Ashley, Alese, and Nick arrived, trampling through the living room to welcome me home. Their excitement fizzled as they turned the corner to my bedroom and caught a glimpse of what I looked like: a wrapped-up mummy. Ashley and Alese inched forward to give me a hug, but Nick—cautious and fearful—lingered in the doorway.

"It's all right, Nicky," I encouraged him. "You can come over."

My voice helped him overcome his shock at the sight of me. He ran over with open arms and gave me a giant hug.

Throughout the day, friends, neighbors, and synagogue congregants brought over meals, pies, brownies, and tall vases of flowers. I was overjoyed by the love, affection, and generosity, but the flood of people was also a bit overwhelming.

After taking some time to rest, I stood up on my own and wandered to the front of the apartment.

"Why on earth are you up?" my Mom asked. "You shouldn't be out of bed; you need to be resting."

"I can't..."

"What do you mean?"

"I can't be back there...alone. I'm afraid."

"We're right here. He can't get to you."

"I just can't do it," I admitted. "I prefer to stay in here with everyone."

I set up camp in the living room on my wicker sofa and chair. These $150 items had been all I could afford when we moved into the apartment, but they were the best purchases I'd ever made. It didn't bother me that they weren't the most comfy pieces of furniture. They were *mine,* and they helped me feel safe.

I couldn't begin to think about all the daunting tasks that lay ahead. My body, mind, and spirit all needed time to heal. Meanwhile, in my fragile condition, I had to find some way to support my family.

I always had great faith in my religion and was a dedicated member of the Jacksonville Jewish Center. I knew from the start it was a tight-knit and giving community, but I could never have imagined the extent to which they would assist my family and me in a time of dire need. They didn't just come to our rescue; they restored our lives.

The members at the Jacksonville Jewish Center and Etz Chaim synagogues valued and exemplified a concept known as *tikkun olam:* the act of helping to repair the world. The synagogue members rallied together to provide extensive emotional and monetary support. They purchased groceries and prepared hot meals for us continuously over the course of the next several weeks. They contacted Jewish Family & Community Services, who assigned experienced therapists to us: Erin Gaal and Lisa Haley. Neither ever sent me a bill.

When friends or family were unavailable, they helped provide rides for me to get to my doctor's appointments and usher my kids to and from school and other activities. Later, without my asking, they presented my kids with Hanukkah gifts.

I don't know how we would have gotten by without this wonderful community.

***

Normally, I was thrilled when friends, such as Rhonda, stopped by to see how I was doing. But one of her visits was somewhat ill timed, as she showed up smack in the middle of a heated debate between my Mom and me as we were preparing to remove the bandages from my head.

"Mom, *please*—I have to shower and wash all of this gunk out of my hair," I begged. "I refuse to take another sponge bath."

"You know you can't do it by yourself," my Mom countered.

"Won't you help me?"

"I can't...I just can't wash your hair. It's too upsetting."

"But Mom—"

"I'll do it. I'll help her," Rhonda intervened.

"Are you sure?" my Mom asked in disbelief. I could tell part of her was relieved that she might be off the hook from performing this off-putting chore.

"Absolutely—I'd be honored to do it," Rhonda volunteered.

Rhonda trailed after me into the bathroom and set to work. After guiding me into the bathtub and helping me sit down, she took her time unwrapping the gauze dressing from around my head. She gingerly allowed droplets of warm water to moisten my hair and body. She drizzled shampoo into my contused scalp. She stayed the course while fastidiously picking out the chunks of dried clots and fatty tissue from around the sutures.

Rhonda did not so much as flinch at the grisly sight or the brownish-red water that circled the drain.

***

Later that week, we received an unexpected visitor: one of the policemen who had been on duty the day of the kidnapping. He toted soft drinks and stuffed animals for the kids.

"I came to say how sorry we are," he apologized as I lay on the wicker sofa. "How sorry *I* am."

"What do you mean? You didn't do anything wrong."

"I wasn't able to prevent what happened. We didn't realize how dangerous he was."

"Please," I insisted. "You don't have to apologize. I don't blame you guys. I know all of you did the best you could."

He gritted his teeth like Clint Eastwood in the Dirty Harry movies. "I wish I'd been the shooter that day. The outcome would've been very different for him."

I sat back to fully absorb what he was saying.

I never forgot that officer because he had taken the time on his own to check up on us. Although he and other officers felt guilt and remorse at not having done more to help me, I never shared that sentiment. The Jacksonville Police Department always showed up in timely fashion when I needed them. They worked tirelessly to stop the harassment within the confines of the law—but, in my opinion, there really wasn't much else they could have done.

On November 7, Detective Royal called to ask if I was willing and able to ride with him and retrace my steps from the morning of the kidnapping. Although I was far from one hundred percent, I didn't hesitate to accept his invitation. I needed to venture outside for fresh air. I also didn't want to risk forgetting any details that might have been important for the police investigation.

He picked up my Mom and me in his unmarked police cruiser and drove to all the spots that were all too familiar to me, beginning at Arrowhead Drive and out onto San Jose Boulevard. We headed onto the small service road behind the Taco Bell. Fragments of horrific memories from that fateful day flooded my mind as Detective Royal exited the car.

He walked around a bit until he found and collected various pieces of evidence, including the discarded hubcap. Further down the block he spotted a black truck that fit the description I had provided. He approached the owner and asked him if he had offered assistance to a man changing a flat tire on a red Neon back on October 27. The man turned out to be the right guy: He confirmed every detail of his exchange with Chris.

We next returned to the gas station where Chris had purchased the oil. The Detective spoke with the cashier— who remembered us having been there—and then checked out the pay phone, which still didn't function.

From there, we made our way to the Winn-Dixie. Of course, the pay phone inside the supermarket worked fine. None of the employees there seemed to remember having seen Chris or me, which wasn't the least bit surprising; they may not have even been any of the employees on duty that day.

Our final stop: the subdivision of new homes that were under construction, where the worst moments of my life had occurred. My spirits lifted when I was officially introduced to Otis, the construction worker who helped rescue me that day. The other two employees who had been on the scene were there to greet me as well.

"It's really nice to see you," Otis said, embracing me.

"I owe you a debt of gratitude," I said, squeezing him back. "If it hadn't been for you, I wouldn't be alive right now."

We spoke a bit about how my Dad had somehow obtained his phone number and called to personally thank him for having helped me on that fateful day.

Otis shook his head in amazement. "For the life of me, I don't know what caused me to buy coffee and sit in the car at the exact moment you needed me. To tell you the truth, I wasn't even scheduled to work that day!"

It felt good to thank Otis for everything he did for me—especially being in the right place at the right time. I also think I benefited from going to the scenes of the crime and facing my demons head-on.

And yet my ordeal wasn't over—not by a long shot. I had a long way to go in my recovery and, at some point soon, had to find a sustainable job that I could manage in my condition.

I also needed to come to terms with the fact that *he* was still alive—albeit touch and go as a result of his injuries. Part of me longed for him to flat-line, so that the kids and I would not live the rest of our lives looking over our shoulders. Another part of me sought to have my day in court and bring him to justice.

To accomplish this, though, I would have to relive my entire trauma in front of a judge, jury, his family, my family, and a courtroom full of media and observers. I was haunted by what he had done to me and could not wrap my head around why someone would attempt to take another person's life when his own is not threatened.

Am I really up for this?

Chapter Sixteen

Led by Detective Royal, the police progressed with their investigation. They photographed and diagramed the crime scenes and retrieved piles of evidence from there, as well as from the impounded Saturn, the woods, and Chris's apartment. Among the objects related to my case gathered in evidence and placed in the police property room: a gold bracelet (Chris's), a gold frog charm (mine), and a bloodstained shovel. Blood was swabbed on the curb, on a manhole cover, on the floor of the garage where I was first struck, and on the front and back left tires of my car. Inside Chris's apartment they discovered VCR tapes, cassette tapes, and a cassette converter—all of which he'd used for stalking purposes. They also removed various items of clothing—including a pair of shorts—and a bloody slat from a vertical blind.

Chris's tenuous health situation no doubt played a large role in the stretched out legal timetable. For better or for worse, he pulled through—despite the severity of the gunshot wounds and knife cuts. Ultimately, the mounting evidence and eyewitness accounts were incontrovertible, and he was charged with armed kidnapping, sexual battery, and attempted first-degree murder. There is no telling what his attorney thought could be used in his defense, but he pled "not guilty." O. David Barksdale, the Assistant State

Attorney, division chief, and member of the Homicide Team, was assigned to build the State's case against him.

Seven months passed, during which time numerous discovery interviews, subpoenas, court filings, motions, and deliberations took place behind the scenes. During this time, I was aware that Chris had improved enough to be released from the hospital and get turned over to police custody. Before he was scheduled to appear in front of a judge and jury, I was notified by Dan Wilensky that the terms of the divorce needed to be settled.

Chris's attorney, Rudy Bolinger, attempted to stall the divorce proceedings to improve his client's chances of getting a reduced prison sentence when the time came. Dan and I wouldn't put up with any of that and forced the meeting on May 27, 1998.

I hadn't seen or spoken to Chris since October 27, 1997. I had no idea what he looked like or if he'd sustained any long-term permanent injuries, and I certainly didn't care. But, in the days building up to that encounter, all kinds of irrational and imagined terrors manifested in my head.

What if he manipulates to get some form of visitation with the children? What if he once again slithers through the system and gets away with everything he's done to me? What if he comes after me again?

No. Impossible. This time he went too far and there is too much incriminating evidence against him. There is no way he is going to be able to see the children or get off scot-free. This time he will get the justice he deserves. He is going to get locked up for good.

I arrived at the courthouse with Dan and Erin, my therapist. She provided essential emotional support for me as we sat in the hallway on a wooden bench and waited to be called in.

When Dan stepped away for a few minutes, Mr. Bolinger paced back-and-forth while muttering proposed terms of the divorce. He had the *chutzpah* to believe his client had something to negotiate! He demanded the following conditions: grandparent rights and shared legal custody of the kids.

I couldn't even look at a man who would contend that such a monster deserved such outrageous things. Outside the obvious fact that Chris had committed heinous crimes, he was looking at serving many years in prison. Why did we even need to talk about legal custody? We had no assets whatsoever. The only thing left? The children. If he were to survive incarceration, at the earliest he would not see the light of day until Nick was a full-grown man in his early twenties.

"I don't understand what there is to talk about," I murmured to Erin, who nodded. She, too, didn't know what to make of this. She held my hand as if to say, *Hang in there*.

Suddenly, rather than speaking through my attorney, Mr. Bolinger pranced over to our bench. He addressed me directly, which was a clear break in protocol. He should have spoken to my attorney, who was present but a distance away from us. "Would you agree to joint legal custody?"

I was dumbfounded. "*Joint legal custody? With Chris*? What exactly does that mean?"

"You would have to discuss all important matters regarding the kids with him. For example, any educational, medical, or other serious issues that might come up—both of you would have to agree."

"Why are you talking to me? I have an attorney," I spat. "But it doesn't make any difference anyway. It's all *no*."

"It never hurts to ask," he shrugged.

As Mr. Bolinger pussyfooted away, I vented to Erin: "Can you believe the nerve of that slime bucket asking if I would consult with Chris on every major decision about my children? Didn't he lose that right when he tried to kill me?"

Erin nodded in stupefaction as Dan approached us. Before I had a chance to convey to him what had just happened, he blurted, "Monique—this is your chance to confront Chris. It's unlikely you'll ever get another one."

I sighed. This moment was inevitable. Dan and Erin had been nudging me to do this for some time. I shuddered, unsure if I was up to it. I deliberated on the decision for a full hour.

"Erin, what do you think?"

"I think you should say what you want to say, and now is the time to do it."

"Will you come with me?"

"Of course."

I made up my mind to press ahead. I just had one question for him to answer.

Dan directed Erin and me into a private, stuffy room filled with bulky leather-bound books on mahogany shelves. We sat at a stately, lengthy table that would separate him from me by about four feet. I held my breath as we waited.

The door opened and he entered, escorted by a towering, armed marshal.

After all these months had elapsed, I couldn't believe it was really *Chris*. It seemed like a lifetime ago that this bastard had ruined my life—and nearly claimed it. It was him, yet it wasn't him. He seemed older, weaker, haggard—a shell of the aggressive predator who had clubbed me mercilessly with a shovel. I was caught off guard by his appearance in the neon orange jumpsuit and rattling chains as he shuffled to the other side of the table and sat down. The marshal hovered over him with folded arms, wary that the prisoner might say or do something out of line.

Everything came back to me: the beating, the abduction, the reckless drive, the sexual assaults, the walk into the garage, the shovel bearing down on me, the limp journey on his shoulder into the woods…. I thought I would never come out of there alive.

I wrestled to control my tears.

Stop. You can do this. You are strong. He is nothing.

I heaved my chest, raised my chin, and looked him straight in the eye. I was ready to hammer him with my one question: "Why did you try to kill me?"

He didn't hesitate for the slightest second, not even checking with his attorney before opening his mouth in ardent denial: "I didn't."

No way. You do not get to lie about this. Not to my face.

"*Yes, you did,*" I asseverated. "You kept me there while I did nothing except try to help you. You beat me in the head with a shovel. As I lay there clinging for life, you leaned over and asked, 'Can you hear me?' Then you felt my neck for a pulse. You told me that I was still alive. You walked around me, moved my hands, and continued whacking my head with a shovel. I played dead. You examined me one more time before walking away and tossing the shovel. You left me presuming I was dead."

No response. I had to prod an acknowledgement of what he had done to me. Something. Anything. There had to be some kind of human being left inside him that I could reach.

"I just want to know *why*. I would never have hurt you. I just wanted a divorce, that's it."

This pushed him over the edge. He began to cry. I wasn't certain if it was because he felt remorse or the fact that he had been caught and was facing the stiff consequences. Still, he didn't say a word.

No matter. I was satisfied; I had received what I had come for.

I exhaled a sigh of relief at having said my piece. I turned to Erin, who was looking down at her hands and sobbing uncontrollably.

Later that day, we signed the final dissolution of our marriage document that included full legal and physical custody of my children, child support (which would never be paid), and grandparents' rights for Chris's parents. The divorce decree also included the exact words from the Lifetime Injunction for Protection issued by Judge Lance

Day on the day I was kidnapped as a reminder that, according to the law, the protections must follow me forever. Part of the document read:

The husband is hereby permanently restrained and enjoined from committing assault, aggravated assault, battery, aggravated battery, sexual battery, or stalking, as well as any other criminal offense resulting in injury or death to Wife.

Amen.

***

June 23, 1998.

Chris caved and entered a plea bargain, admitting he was guilty of kidnapping to commit or facilitate the commission of a felony with a firearm, sexual battery, attempted first degree domestic murder, and aggravated assault. His bond had already been forfeited, costing his parents ownership of their house.

Although Chris's parents were convinced, I was the one who had proposed the thirty-year sentencing term, it was O. David Barksdale who had done so. My former in-laws begged me not to ask for the maximum sentence for Chris. David explained to them that he was prosecuting the case, not me, and the State of Florida would determine the sentence.

My ex-husband and the father of my children accepted a plea bargain of twenty-six years, requiring him to serve eighty percent of that behind bars.

Justice.

***

Although I finally had closure regarding my marriage, I was far from out of the woods when it came to the aftermath of these cataclysmic events. Aside from the continuing medical treatments and therapies—both emotional and physical—I still had to contend with my job situation and the mounting bills. I was filing weekly unemployment, but I needed to find work as soon as possible. I'd hoped to find a job where they would pay for additional training to further my education and expand my career opportunities.

I considered taking a medical transcription course through Medical Transcription, Inc., so I could work from home and feed my internal need for medical jargon. I learned that the next class—a ten-week intensive course conducted Monday through Friday, 8:30 a.m. to 5 p.m.—started in January. The cost was $1,000 plus $250 in medical reference books and dictionaries. After much thought, I realized my hands and fingers needed a lot more healing before I could even consider training for a job involving extensive typing, but I was determined to take the course.

Once again I had to be creative and proactive for my family to survive financially. I had never received a single dime of child support from Chris during the nine months of separation, even though the Navy had paid him over $1,400 per month to support his wife and dependents.

I sought assistance by contacting the Navy-Marine Corps Relief Society (NMCRS). A kind woman from that office empathized with my situation and helped me collect $363—not much, but it was something. Later, her continued efforts provided us with an additional few hundred dollars.

I then filled out the requisite forms with the Office of the Attorney General, Department of Legal Affairs, Tallahassee, Florida, to apply for victim's reimbursement. I qualified to receive $732 compensation—enough to cover rent—since I had suffered a physical injury as a result of a crime.

Somehow, thanks to these modest amounts and the food we received from the community, we were able to scrape by.

Even so, I was done with Jacksonville. I had several close friends, loved the synagogue, and appreciated everything they had done for my family. But I was ready for a fresh start. I didn't want to forever be looked upon as a victim and needed new surroundings for the kids and myself.

I weighed my options, starting with the obvious one: San Diego. It made some sense in that it was familiar to me, but it also conjured up memories of my early days with Chris. I understood that, if we were to move there, Chris's parents would insist upon being heavily involved in the kids' lives. I didn't mind them at all; my issue was more about Chris. I knew that even from prison he would pressure his parents for a blow-by-blow account of my family's every move. I was not going to allow any part of that to happen: As far as I was concerned, he was gone from our lives.

I received a timely call from an old friend, Rabbi Adler, who had relocated with his wife and family to West Hartford, Connecticut, a couple of years earlier. I had remained in occasional contact with them during this time. I missed chatting and learning with his wife, Leslie.

"Monique," he proposed, "Why not move to West Hartford? There is a Solomon Schechter Day School here, many synagogues, readily available kosher foods, and lots of activities for the kids."

First the West Coast, next Japan, and then the South. Now the Northeast? Well…why not? I had always been enamored with New England—its deep colonial history, quaint towns, magnificent four seasons, and richness of higher education. Plus, my Uncle Rodney lived in Boston, which isn't a far drive from West Hartford.

My Dad was a voice of reason: "You can't just decide to move somewhere without having visited the place. At least go and see it first."

After my Dad offered to reimburse me for the $200 airfare, I flew off to Connecticut. The rabbi and rebbetzin hosted me and showed me around town. I fell in love with

West Hartford and made up my mind on the spot: We would relocate as soon as the kids finished school that year.

Of course, there was still one crucial matter: how I was going to afford the move. I spent endless nights wrangling over my ability to pull this off.

Since the Navy declined to compensate me for the money Chris had hoarded, I decided to take them on. I reached out to the Honorable Tillie Fowler, member, United States House of Representatives. Congresswoman Fowler responded to me: "To be of help to you, I have contacted the Department of the Navy concerning the matter of dependent support and to let the admiral know of my concern in the matter. When information is received from the Navy, I will forward it to you."

She and her staff wrote numerous additional letters and made several phone calls advocating on my behalf to the naval base and then to Washington, D.C.

Their efforts paid off. In May 1998, I received a letter from the Department of the Navy in Washington, D.C. stating they were granting a year's worth of back pay in the form of transitional compensation totaling $17,940.

Not only did that check allow me to catch up the months of overdue living expenses and bills, it provided the necessary three months' rental deposit with enough left over for us to live on until I could find steady employment. On top of that, through letter exchanges between the rear admiral of Chris's naval base and me, I convinced the Navy to cover our moving expenses—something I felt entitled to since they would do it for any other military family.

Thank God!

Alive. It feels so good to be alive.

Epilogue

Earl ("Earle") Faison: My Dad was inducted into the San Diego Chargers Hall of Fame, the Indiana University Hall of Fame, the San Diego Hall of Champions, Breitbard Hall of Fame, and the Virginia Hall of Fame. He was named a member of the San Diego Chargers 50th Anniversary Team. Though he was beloved by football fans and teammates and inspired many students as an educator, he and I were never able to grow as close as I would have liked. He passed away on June 12, 2016, at seventy-seven years of age in Prescott, Arizona. He was described in his *Newport News* obituary as a "gentle giant."

Barbara Jewel Marshall: My Mom is seventy-nine years old, retired, and healthy. She is a senior member of the Institute of Industrial and Systems Engineers. She has remained sober for over forty-six years and has helped dozens of people gain and maintain their sobriety as a sponsor and active leader with Alcoholics Anonymous. She is an active alumna of Ohio State. She is also a breast cancer survivor. Retired in Connecticut, she continues to be a major positive force in my life.

Rodney Marshall: Uncle Rodney continues to reside in the Boston area, although he is bedridden due to a series of strokes. We remain close and I visit him as often as I can.

Rosa and Mario Rodriguez *(names changed)*: To the best of my knowledge, they lost ownership of their home from having posted bail for their son. Rosa passed away from a massive heart attack approximately sixteen months after my kidnapping. Last I was aware, Mario—as well his daughter, Chris's sister—were alive and well.

Ashley: My eldest daughter received her Bachelor of Science, Nursing, and is an ICU nurse dedicated to cardiac critical care. Ashley's travels have taken her within the United States and abroad to Israel, Nicaragua, and various locations in Spain. She is extremely protective of the family and always rushes to assist her siblings and me whenever we are in need. She is married and recently started a family.

Alese: My middle child graduated from Miss Porter's, attended an Ivy League college, and then graduated from law school. She now serves as a corporate lawyer in a city she loves. Alese's studies and leisure time have allowed her to travel to Israel, China, the Czech Republic, and Vienna. Although she appreciates her space and downtime, she has always been there for her siblings and me in difficult and joyful times.

Nick: Post high school graduation, my son completed a GAP year by working with City Year, an AmeriCorps program working with middle school students. He attended college and continues his passion for lacrosse as both a player and youth coach. He enjoys working for an established company in a large city. Nick's love of adventure has taken him to London and Denmark. As the only man in the family, he worries about all of us and is always ready to jump to our aide when needed.

Lillian: Thankfully, my youngest daughter was not born when the events of this book took place. I have worked tirelessly to instill a healthy amount of caution while trying not to allow my past to terrify her. She has only begun to hear the events of her family's history. I have told her countless times to always follow her gut, I hope it sticks. Lillian's travels have taken her to Israel with more to come.

Monique Faison Ross: Barrington and I married not long after the family's move to Connecticut. Together we adopted a five-week-old child, Lillian. I knew my family was complete the moment I held her in my arms. My marriage to Barrington ended in an amicable divorce.

I discovered later in life that choosing a partner for me was not based on gender.

In 2012, with the full support of my four children, I married a woman named Leah. It was our Conservative synagogue's first same sex marriage in its then ninety-five-year history.

I continue to suffer from daily PTSD but refuse to permit these issues to define my life or that of my children. We are all extremely cautious people, regularly looking over our shoulders to see if anything is out of the ordinary, i.e., a car following us.

I live a full life and will never allow my traumatic experience to hold me back in any way, despite the frightening visions that regularly race through my mind. Soon Lillian will be heading off to college, at which point Leah and I will be empty nesters. I look forward to focusing on my volunteer and advocacy work.

I am often asked, "Is writing cathartic for you?"

Unfortunately, telling this story has never helped me. Even today, it is like those events happened yesterday. I work hard—often failing—to keep the paranoid visions at bay.

Barrington Walker *(name changed)*: Barrington and I were married for ten years, during which time we adopted Lillian. As with Chris, I supported his further education. He served in the insurance industry and later shifted to working with veterans. We divorced with shared custody of our child. He has since remarried.

Christopher (Chris) Rodriquez *(name changed)*: Chris survived prison. After the initial plea bargain, he spent his time convincing a public defender and then a judge that he deserved a trial to have his case reheard. To avoid taking my children out of school and college for a trial, I followed O. David Barksdale's guidance and agreed to a reduced sentence of twenty years. This entitled Chris to serve eighty percent of that term, and he was released from prison in 2014. Due to my lifetime Injunction for Protection, he is prohibited from having any contact with me for the remainder of my life, directly or through a third party. My family has had no contact with him during his imprisonment or since his release, and we plan to keep it that way. I changed Chris's name to avoid poking the lion in any fashion that might provoke retaliation.

A Note on Other Names

Wherever possible, names have been retained with permission. However, the following names were changed out of respect for the privacy of the individuals and their families (or the names have faded from my memory):

- Pat and Jack (friends)
- Todd and Stacy (cousins)
- Allison (Chris's high school girlfriend)
- Grady O'Neill (neighbor)
- Commanders Franks and Harry Storch
- Claire (Chris's later girlfriend)
- Rudy Bolinger (Chris's attorney)

Appendix A: If You Need Assistance

National Coalition Against Domestic Violence

The mission of the National Coalition Against Domestic Violence (NCADV) is to lead, mobilize, and raise their voices to support efforts that demand a change of conditions that lead to domestic violence, such as patriarchy, privilege, racism, sexism, and classism. They are dedicated to supporting survivors and holding offenders accountable and supporting advocates.

Contact:
One Broadway Suite B210
Denver, CO 80203
(303) 839-1852
https://ncadv.org

Power and Control Wheel

The Power and Control Wheel was created in Duluth, Minnesota, by working with women who were attending support and education groups for survivors of domestic violence. Over time, they described what we now see as the tactics on the Power and Control Wheel. The ones chosen for the wheel were those most universally experienced by women living with abusers. It is a powerful tool that helps people see the patterns in behavior and name the violence that has been used against them.

DOMESTIC ABUSE INTERVENTION PROGRAMS
202 East Superior Street
Duluth, Minnesota 55802
218-722-2781
www.theduluthmodel.org

The "Power and Control Wheel" represents the power and control tactics used by an abusive person (i.e., intimate partner, family member, neighbor, or co-worker). These methods can often be subtle and difficult to recognize and do not always include physical violence. This wheel shows how easily one can end up feeling trapped in an unhealthy situation. Be aware that there are professionals available who can provide confidential guidance to assist you. Image used with permission from the Domestic Abuse Intervention Programs. (c) Copyright, all rights reserved.

Contact:

DOMESTIC ABUSE INTERVENTION PROGRAMS
202 East Superior Street Duluth, Minnesota 55802
218-722-2781
www.theduluthmodel.org

Appendix B: Documents

The documents from Appendix B can also be viewed by visiting: *http://wbp.bz/playingdeadgallery*

IN THE CIRCUIT COURT, FOURTH
JUDICIAL CIRCUIT, IN AND FOR
DUVAL COUNTY, FLORIDA.

A TRUE COPY HEREOF
IN ABOVE CASE SIGNED

CASE NO: ███████████
DIVISION: FM-V

OCT 28 1997

IN RE: THE MARRIAGE OF

signature
CIRCUIT COURT JUDGE

MONIQUE ███████ Wife

and

████████████████, Husband

SECOND AMENDED FINAL JUDGMENT ON INJUNCTION FOR PROTECTION AGAINST DOMESTIC VIOLENCE

THIS CAUSE came on to be heard on October 27, 1997 upon the Wife's oral motion to modify the Amended Final Judgment on Injunction for Protection Against Domestic Violence entered in this cause. Daniel F. Wilensky appeared by telephone as counsel for the Wife. ████████ ████████ appeared by telephone as counsel for the Husband. The Court having been fully advised in the premises, thereupon

ORDERED AND ADJUDGED that:

1. The Respondent/Husband, ████████████████ shall have **no contact** **whatsoever** with his minor children, to wit: ALESE ████████, born ██████████, NICHOLAS ███████, born ██████████, and ASHLEY ███████, born ██████████, until further Order of the Court. No contact means he shall not contact his children in person, by mail, by telephone or through a third party.

2. The Respondent/Husband is enjoined and restrained from committing any acts of violence against the Petitioner/Wife. Violence includes any assault, aggravated assault, battery, aggravated battery, sexual battery or stalking, as well as any other criminal offense resulting in injury or death to the Petitioner.

3. The Respondent shall stay at least 500 feet away from Petitioner/Wife's residence, the grounds of Petitioner/Wife's apartment complex, and Petitioner/Wife's place of employment.

1

4. The Respondent shall not go to, in or near the Petitioner's current or any subsequent place of employment.

5. The Respondent/Husband shall have no contact with the Petitioner/Wife in person, by mail, by telephone, or through a third party.

This Final Judgment is valid throughout the State of Florida and shall be enforced by law enforcement authorities. The Jacksonville Sheriff's Office, the Sheriffs of the State of Florida, their Deputies, and law enforcement officers of the jurisdiction in which a violation of this injunction occurs, shall enforce the provisions of this Order, and are authorized to arrest for any violation of those provisions of this Order.

If Respondent/Husband is arrested and charged with violation of this judgment, he shall be brought before the Honorable Lance Day, instanter, by the Office of the Sheriff, then to show cause why he should not be adjudged in contempt of Court and punished accordingly for violation of the Orders of this Court

This Order takes precedence over and **supercedes all prior Orders** of this Court entered in Case No.: ▮▮▮▮▮ , Division: FM-V, and Case No.: ▮▮▮▮▮ FM, Division: FM-F. This Order shall remain in full force and effect until modified by a subsequent Order of this Court.

ORDERED AND ADJUDGED this _____ day of October, 1997.   OCT 28 1997
                                                          NPT 10-27-97

_____
CIRCUIT JUDGE   CIRCUIT COURT JUDGE

Copies to:

Daniel F. Wilensky, Esquire
1916 Atlantic Boulevard
Jacksonville, Florida 32207

Monique ▮▮▮▮▮
Jacksonville, FL 32257

2

1. Amended Final Injunction (Redacted). As a result of the kidnapping, Judge Lance Day immediately ordered an amended Final Injunction for Protection. In Monique's divorce decree it was changed to a lifetime term.

2. Police Report: October 27, 2019 (Redacted). The heavily marked up first page of the official police arrest and booking report citing all of the crimes committed during Monique's kidnapping.

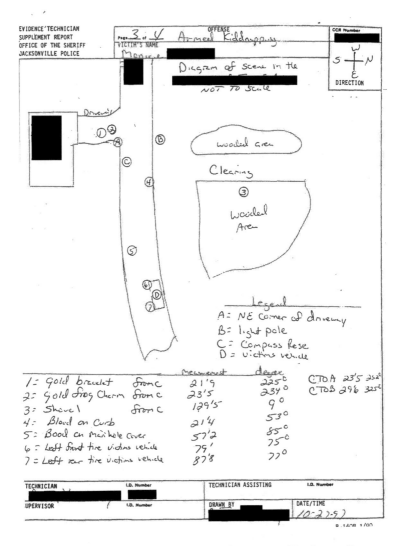

Page 3 of √

OFFENSE Armed Kiddnapping

CCR Number

VICTIM'S NAME Monique

DIRECTION

Diagram of Scene in the

NOT TO Scale

Driveway

① ②
Ⓐ
Ⓑ
Ⓒ
Ⓓ

Wooded area

Clearing

③

Wooded Area

Ⓔ

⑥
Ⓓ
⑦

Legend
A = NE Corner of driveway
B = light pole
C = Compass Rose
D = Victims vehicle

measurement / degree

				measurement	degree	
1 =	Gold bracelet	from c		21'9	225°	C TO A 23'5 252°
2 =	Gold frog Charm	from c		23'5	234°	C TO B 296 325°
3 =	Shovel	from c		129'5	9°	
4 =	Blood on Curb			21'4	53°	
5 =	Bood on manhole cover			57'2	85°	
6 =	Left front tire victims vehicle			79'	75°	
7 =	Left rear tire victims vehicle			87'8	77°	

TECHNICIAN	I.D. Number	TECHNICIAN ASSISTING	I.D. Number
UPERVISOR	I.D. Number	DRAWN BY	DATE/TIME 10-27-97

P 1408 1/00

3. Police Crime Scene Diagram (Redacted).
This police sketch outlines the crime scene in the woods where Monique was struck several times and played dead.

SA# ███████   Div: CR-B/SAD

JACKSONVILLE FIRE AND RESCUE
107 N. MARKET ST. 32202
JACKSONVILLE, FLORIDA 32202
(904)-630-2463
EMS AGENCY: JACKSONVILLE FIRE AND RESCUE   ID:1605
INCIDENT DATE: 10/27/97
AGENCY INCIDENT NUMBER: ███

PATIENT 1 OF 1 TOTAL PATIENTS
UNIT NAME: RESCUE ███ ████████████

NAME: ████████ , MONIQUE
DATE OF BIRTH: AGE: 31 YEARS

NARRATIVE:

PT FOUND SITTING IN AUTO. WAS BROUGHT TO OUR LOCATION BY A CONSTRUCTION
WORKER WHO FOUND HER WALKING OUT OF WOODS NEAR HIS WORKSITE. FOUND AWAKE,
BLOODY, WOUNDS TO HEAD SHE SAID HER HUSBAND INFLICTED WITH A SHOVEL. PT.
PALE, WEAK, NO PALP. EXT. PULSES. BP NOT READABLE. SWELLING TO BOTH HANDS
WITH POSS FX. TRAUMA ALERT CALLED AND LIFE FLIGHT ENROUTE. SALINE IV EST.
OPEN. BOTH HANDS SPLINTED, CID AND BANDAGED. WOUNDS IN HEAD APPEARED MULT
AND THROUGHT SKULL. TRANS. TO UHJ VIA LIFE FLIGHT.

ASSESSMENT:
AIRWAY: PATENT   BREATHING EXPANSION: EQUAL EXPANSION
BREATH SOUNDS: (L) CLEAR TO AUSCULTATION   (R) CLEAR TO AUSCULTATION
BREATH STATUS: EQUAL

SKIN TEMP: NORMAL   COLOR: PALE   MOISTURE: NORMAL

LEFT EYE SIZE: NORMAL   REACTS
RIGHT EYE SIZE: NORMAL   REACTS

GCS   EYES: 3 TO SPEECH   VERBAL: 5 ORIENTED   MOTOR: 6 OBEYS
TOTAL: 14

PULSES: RADIAL: NO   CAROTID: YES   OTHER:
WEAK,REGULAR
CAPILLARY REFILL: GREATER THAN 2 SECONDS

TRAUMA:
DATE OF INJURY: 10/27/97
TIME OF INJURY: 14:00
INJURY SITES: HEAD: PENETRATE;   HEAD: LACERATION;   LEFT HAND: OTHER;
RIGHT HAND: OTHER;   FACE: CONTUSE
MECHANISM OF INJURY: ASSAULT
TRAUMA ALERT CALLED: YES
CRITERION 1: SBP < 90
CRITERION 2:
TRAUMA PROTOCOL EXCEPTION:

VITAL SIGNS:
TIME	PULSE	RESP	SBP/DBP	RHYTHM	SAO2	BLD SUGAR	PULSES	ECTOPY
14:47	100	20	0 0		85		YES	
15:12	100	20	100 0		90		YES	

IV/IO FLUIDS:
AN IV LINE OF NORMAL SALINE WAS STARTED IN THE LEFT ANTECUBITAL FOSSA AFTER
3 ATTEMPTS.
       (18 GUAGE CATHETER) (500 CCS TOTAL) (WIDE OPEN) ███████

```
(PARAMEDIC) ████████

MEDICATIONS:

INTERVENTIONS:
    POSITION BY . ( AFTER  ATTEMPTS)
    SAO2 BY .  ( AFTER  ATTEMPTS)
    OXYGEN BY .  ( AFTER  ATTEMPTS)
    NON-REBREATHER MASK BY . ( AFTER  ATTEMPTS)
    CARDIAC MONITORING BY . ( AFTER  ATTEMPTS)
    BANDAGE BY . ( AFTER  ATTEMPTS)
        CID BY .
    SPLINT / TRACTION SPLINT BY . ( AFTER  ATTEMPTS)

INCIDENT INFORMATION:
INCIDENT LOCATION: ████████████████
NATURE OF CALL AS DISPATCHED: UNKNOWN
DELAY TO SCENE: NONE    DELAY FROM SCENE: NONE
NATURE OF CALL AT SCENE: TRAUMA CALL


DISPOSITION: TRANSPORT VIA AIR TO UNIVERSITY MEDICAL CENTER - JAX 11613
(REASON DESTINATION CHOSEN: PER PROTOCOL)
TYPE OF EXPOSURE ON THIS RUN: NONE


LEAD CREW MEMBER: ████████████████████████
CREW MEMBER 2: ████████████████████

CALL RECEIVED 14:42      DISPATCH 14:42          DEPART 14:42
ARRIVE LOC 14:45         PATIENT CONTACT 14:46    START EXTRICATION
END EXTRICATION      TRAUMA ALERT CALLED 14:47 TRANSPORT ARRIVED 15:05
PT. DEPARTS 15:13        UNIT DEPARTS 15:18       ARRIVE DEST.
AVAILABLE 15:35

RESPONSE TO SCENE: EMERGENCY       RESPONSE FROM SCENE: N/A
CALL LEVEL: ALS
HOW EMS ACCESSED: UNKNOWN

MILEAGE:   DISPATCH:    TOTAL MILES

ASSSISTING:  JACKSONVILLE FIRE AND RESCUE  ENGINE ██ , JACKSONVILLE SHERIFFS
OFFICE; LIFE FLIGHT - BMC  HELICOPTER

PATIENT INFORMATION:
NAME: ████████  MONIQUE
DATE OF BIRTH:     AGE:  31  YEARS
RACE:  BLACK   SEX:  FEMALE
SOCIAL SECURITY NUMBER:
DRIVER'S LICENSE:
ADRESS: UNKNOWN  UNKNOWN      CITY:  JACKSONVILLE
STATE: FLORIDA    ZIP:  UNKNOWN    PHONE:  904-
PRIVATE PHYSICIAN:

CURRENT MEDICATIONS: UNKNOWN
ALLERGIES: UNKNOWN
PAST MEDICAL HISTORY: UNKNOWN

BILLING INFORMATION:
WORK RELATED: NO

SIGNATURES:

CREW SIGNATURE: ████████████ (PARAMEDIC) ████████ (ELECTRONIC SIGNATURE)
```

4. Fire and Rescue Report (Redacted).

Jacksonville Fire and Rescue were the first responders to arrive at the scene and treat Monique after Otis assisted her. They itemized their findings in this report and called in the helicopter team, Life Flight, who took Monique to the hospital by helicopter.

UNIVERSITY
MEDICAL
CENTER U
University of Florida Urban Campus

MONIQUE
10-27-97 8F31Y YRS
LANPARD,SIMO/
S

TRAUMA ADMISSION TRANSFER ORDERS

ADMIT TO: [] Surgical ICU [X] Surgical Stepdown [] Post Trauma [] Trauma Service
ADMITTING PHYSICIAN _Lamphart, Bradley_
DIAGNOSIS _basilar skull fx_
MECHANISM _assault & closed — pt patient_
INJURIES _basilar skull fracture_
CONDITION [] Critical [] Critical but stable [X] Serious [] Fair [] Good
CONSULTS _Neurosurgery & OMF_
ALLERGIES _NKDA_
VITAL SIGNS Q _4_ H NEURO CHECK Q _4_ H VASCULAR CHECK TO ____ Q ____ H
ACTIVITY: _Bed rest, C-Collar_

NURSING

[] NG to low intermittant suction
[] Foley to bedside drain
[] NG/DHT flushes Q 4 H with tap water
[X] Sequential compression hose
[X] Aspen collar ____
[] Specialty bed ____
[] Cooling blanket for temp > ____ °F
[] IV fluids: _N.S. bolus 1L then ± N.S. +20KCl @ 100cc/_°
[X] Diet: _NPO except_ (ice)
[X] Wound Care: _Pressure bandage to scalp_

[] Chest tube to: ____ suction ____ water seal
[] JP to ____ suction
[] Incentive spirometer Q1 H while awake with assistance
[] Soft restraints prn

MEDICATIONS: Circle appropriate route

[X] Heparin 5000 units sq BID
[] Sucralfate 1 gram po/NG Q 6 H
[X] Acetaminophen 650 mg elixir/po/pr Q4 H prn for headache or temp > ___ ° F
[X] Morphine _4_ mg IV/IM prn pain Q _/_ H
[] Tylox ___ po Q ___ H prn pain
[X] Diazepam _5_ mg IV/IM prn agitation Q _6_ H
[] Docusate 240 mg po BID prn constipation
[X] Other: _Ancef 1 gram iv q 8° x 3_

[] Nizatidine 150 mg po/NG BID
[] Maalox TC 15cc prn for NG pH <5.0 Q4 H
[X] Promethazine _2.5_ mg IV/IM prn for nausea Q _6_ H
[] See PCA sheet
[] Bisacodyl 5 mg po or 10 mg PR prn constipation
[] Antibiotics: ____

[X] X-ray _H&H CBC @ 2200_
[X] Labs: _H & H @ 2200_
[] Accuchecks Q ___ H call for blood sugar > ____ or < ____
[] Physiatry consult
[] Physical Therapy Consult   [] Physical Therapy in Department   [] Occupational Therapy Consult
[] Speech Therapy Consult   [] Nutrition Consult   [X] Social Services Consult
Vent Settings: Mode ____ Rate ____ Tidal Volume ____ FiO2 ____ PEEP ____
[X] Continuous Pulse Oximetry   [] Continuous EKG Monitoring
Call trauma house officer for HR > _110_ or < _60_, SBP > _150_ or < ___, DBP > _40_ or ____
temp > _101_/F, RR > _20_ or < _8_, urine output < _40_ cc/hour, or any acute neurological changes

Signature ████████   Number _2253_   Date/Time _10/27/97_

This is to certify that inpatient hospital services are needed ____
Date ____   Physician Signature ____

6062-008 3/96

5. Medical Report University Hospital Trauma Admission (Redacted).
Monique's detailed medical admission form to University Medical Center, Trauma Admission. While in the hospital, Monique underwent a battery of tests, including X-rays of fingers and hands; CT scans of the skull; and lab work to assess internal damage.

DEPARTMENT OF THE NAVY
NAVAL AIR STATION
JACKSONVILLE, FLORIDA 32212-5000

Mrs. Monique ███████████
Jacksonville, FL 32257

Dear Mrs. ██████,

This is in response to your letter to Rear Admiral ████████ Commander, Naval Base Jacksonville, dated June 24, 1998, regarding allegations concerning the conduct of one of my officers, Commander ████████████ United States Navy.

I first and foremost want to express my concern for you and your family's welfare under what must have been an extremely difficult personal experience. I can only imagine the difficulties and pain you have endured.

I have reviewed the facts and circumstances regarding your allegations against Commander ████████, specifically, non-payment of financial support for family member and stalking.

It is documented that Mr. ████ was repeatedly counseled concerning his moral obligation to provide financial support. He was instructed to provide proof in the form of receipts and/or canceled checks to substantiate his claim that he was providing for his family in the form of rent and other shared obligations. While I appreciate how difficult this situation was for you, the Department of the Navy has no authority to adjudicate matters of a civil nature. A court order is required to compel a service member to provide payments of alimony and or child support. Commander ████████ never had the authority to enforce the type of payments you were requesting.

As for your allegations of stalking, Commander ████████ employed the services of every resource at his disposal and within the limits of the Navy's jurisdiction, in an attempt to resolve the matter which included his Command Master Chief, Command Judge Advocate, Family Service Center, Naval Hospital Jacksonville and Navy Criminal Investigative Service. These resources, formal counseling sessions, mental health evaluations and a Military Protection Order were all used to resolve the situation but were not enough to deter the determined actions of your former spouse.

   I have concluded that the actions taken and resources used by Commander ████████ were thorough, consistent and in accordance with Navy policy.

                              Sincerely,

                              ████████████████
                              Captain, USN
                              Command Officer

6. Department of the Navy Letter (Redacted). On behalf of the admiral, a captain explained in various letters to Monique and Congresswoman Fowler that the Navy did everything within their power to control Chris—but nothing worked.

The documents from Appendix B can be viewed by visiting: *http://wbp.bz/playingdeadgallery*

ABOUT THE AUTHORS

MONIQUE FAISON ROSS

Monique Faison Ross was born in San Francisco and grew up as an only child in San Diego. She was raised primarily by her mom, Barbara, an industrial engineer. Her father, William Earl (Earle) Faison, was a four-time all-star defensive end for the San Diego Chargers.

Monique has worked as a program manager for a Connecticut educational non-profit since 2004. She has also served in various volunteer roles—from being a board of trustee member to running committees and helping the community in various ways. She recently accepted a seat on the Fatality Review Task Force for Connecticut.

She became an "accidental author" when a group of friends convinced her that she had to tell her story. Her writings have appeared in *Lilith Magazine* and other publications.

Her website and blog may be found here:
https://www.moniquefaisonross.com

Monique, who is married and lives in Connecticut, has four children and a new grandchild.

GARY M. KREBS

Writer, author, literary agent, and former book publisher Gary M. Krebs is the founder of GMK Writing and Editing, Inc. He received his B.F.A. from the Dramatic Writing Program, Tisch School of the Arts (NYU).

Before writing full-time and launching his own business, he was Associate Publisher at Brilliance Publishing (a division of Amazon Publishing); VP, Group Publisher, McGraw-Hill Professional; Group Publisher, Globe Pequot Press; Publisher, Adams Media (a division of F+W Publications); Publishing Director, Rodale; and Publishing Director, Macmillan Publishing. Prior to serving as Publisher, he was an acquisitions editor at several houses and U.S. Editor of *The Guinness Book of Records*.

His credited writings include *Wealth Made Easy* (Dr. Greg S. Reid with Gary M. Krebs), *Creating Sales Stars* (Stephan Schiffman with Gary M. Krebs), *The Rock and Roll Reader's Guide*, and *The Guinness Book of Sports Records*.

Gary lives in Fairfield, CT. His web site may be found here: *https://www.gmkwritingandediting.com/*

His Huffington Post blog may be found here:
http://www.huffingtonpost.com/author/gary-m-krebs

PHOTOS

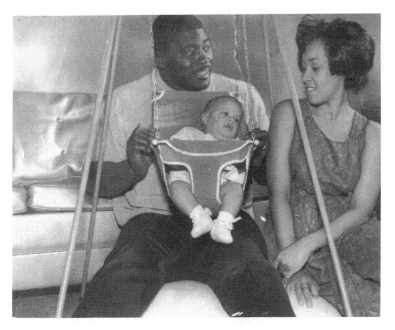

1. Barbara and Earl Faison with their daughter, Monique, in the swing. This image appeared in the San Diego newspaper. *From the collection of Monique Faison Ross.*

2. Earl appeared on several TV shows, including The Six Million Dollar Man. Here he poses with the show's star, Lee Majors. *From the collection of Monique Faison Ross.*

3. Ashley, Alese, and Nick unwrap Chanukah presents in December 1997. The Jewish community was kind enough to help provide gifts for them, since my circumstances prevented me from doing so. *From the collection of Monique Faison Ross.*

4. Monique, her Mom, and the kids in Japan. *From the collection of Monique Faison Ross.*

Police shoot kidnap suspect

By Jim Schoettler
Times-Union staff writer

A Jacksonville man charged with kidnapping, raping and beating his estranged wife was shot by a police officer yesterday after the officer was attacked with a butcher knife, police said.

Officer Michael Perry shot the 32-year-old suspect in the stomach and right foot about 2:30 a.m. while Perry and other officers hunted for him in Monday's kidnapping. The shooting

occurred in the 3900 block of Old Sunbeam Road, said Chief Frank Mackesy of the Jacksonville Sheriff's Office.

The man was in fair condition last night at University Medical Center, where his 31-year-old wife also was hospitalized.

The woman had been left for dead after a four-hour attack that included being bashed in the head with a shovel and raped. The shovel strikes were so hard they damaged the woman's eye sockets, police said.

"It's horrible how bad off she is and

it's amazing she's still alive," said Dan Wilensky, the woman's lawyer, who visited her in the hospital yesterday. "I never had any indication there would be violence like this."

Neither suspect nor victim are being identified by The Florida Times-Union because the newspaper doesn't identify rape victims without their consent.

The man was captured about 19 hours after police say he took his wife from outside her apartment in the 10300 block of Arrowhead Drive East in Mandarin. The kidnapping oc-

curred at gunpoint about 8:30 a.m. Monday in front of the couple's hysterical 4-year-old son and 9-year-old daughter, who fled to a neighbor's house.

"He had his hand covering her mouth and kept saying, 'Shut up,'" said Ann Sims, 56, who watched the abduction from her living room. "I opened the window and screamed at him to let go of her. He hit her once and pushed her in the car. My daugh-

See CHILDREN, Page B-2

5. The Jacksonville *Metro* reported Monique's attack and the police's subsequent shooting of Chris on October 29, 1997.

6. Blood traces found on the curb, where Monique had exited the woods. *Photo taken by the Jacksonville Police photographer.*

7. Blood spatter on the manhole cover, where Monique collapsed after her escape from the woods. *Photo taken by the Jacksonville Police photographer.*

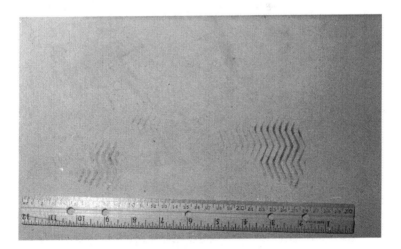

8. Chris's bloodied footprint found in the garage. *Photo taken by the Jacksonville Police photographer.*

9. A pool of blood on the garage floor, where Monique landed after having received the first shovel blow to the head. *Photo taken by the Jacksonville Police photographer.*

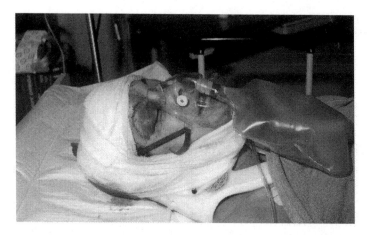

10. ICU headshot of Monique recovering in the hospital after her near-fatal wounds. The injuries to her head included a basilar skull fracture and six centimeter and eight centimeter lacerations to her scalp. *Photo taken by the Jacksonville Police evidence team.*

11. Monique's red Dodge Neon. Visible in the photo is the spare tire on the right front that Chris had changed during the kidnapping. *Photo taken by the Jacksonville Police photographer.*

12. The shovel as it appeared abandoned in the woods. Evidence revealed Monique's blood on the steel. *Photo taken by the Jacksonville Police photographer.*

13. The location where Chris was hiding in the culvert. The evidence markers indicate where he was shot by Officer Perry. *Photo taken by the Jacksonville Police photographer.*

*For More News About Monique Faison Ross
and Gary M. Krebs, Signup For Our Newsletter:*
http://wbp.bz/newsletter

*Word-of-mouth is critical to an author's long-
term success. If you appreciated this book please
leave a review on the Amazon sales page:*
http://wbp.bz/playingdeada

PROLOGUE

I've Seen Where You Live, I Know What You Eat

A tremor went down my spine the day I heard that Leonard was planning to sell his ranch-style house in the New Jersey suburbs and move to my neighborhood, Williamsburg, Brooklyn. It was a gray, chilly spring day, fittingly gloomy. The dank weather compounded my mood and lent itself to a scene from a grainy noir movie, dilapidated factories in stages of decomposition everywhere that he could hide, stash a weapon, stash a body. Stash me.

It seemed that Leonard thought a loft might better suit his lifestyle. Leonard, the schizophrenic child math prodigy, who had blossomed into a wealthy swinger, painter, and collector of sexual paraphernalia. This wasn't a good sign since his present residence had apparently been suitably outfitted for his bacchanals for quite some time. He claimed he wanted something bigger, hipper, something located in an area where he wouldn't stand out quite as much from his cookie cutter neighbors in New Jersey. But I knew that wasn't it. His wealth could have easily afforded him lofts in SoHo, Tribeca, or Chelsea—all within striking distance of the downtown dungeons and secret after-hours places. The real attraction for him was his new "cousin Susan." Was he intent on intensifying the deviant nature of his parties with me as his guest of honor?

I'd never met Leonard, but I knew a lot about him. I knew that he had been charged but never convicted of rape and kidnapping. I knew that he had a lavish psychiatric history and that he often went off his meds and had been repeatedly hospitalized. His doctors had decided that he was mentally competent for release. He had been able to keep down his Wall Street job, at least well enough to amass a fortune. Leonard had the knack of appearing so normal at times, so non-descript. If he wanted to, he could look like an ordinary person. He was just an *ordinary* person, one who just happened to be obsessed with me.

I fearfully imagined him dazed, wandering the streets searching for me. The area could readily conceal someone like Leonard by virtue of the eclectic mix of people it attracted. Much to the chagrin of natives and old timers, the "weird folk" had moved in and found that it suited their alternate lifestyles all too well. Williamsburg. It was a forgotten New York neighborhood with exotic, dark alleys; a Mecca for artists, musicians, yuppies, skinheads, and those of the tattooed persuasion. The hulking smokestack of the Domino Sugar factory belched out an aroma of burned brown sugar that draped everything with a sweet, invisible mist. It was a hipster zone, where a chameleon like Leonard could crawl unobtrusively from building to building, from playground to lounge. Leonard, a master of stealth to begin with, might find that Williamsburg rendered his avant-garde lifestyle and morbid moods virtually invisible.

Early spring in New York City can be depressing, and the gloomy weekend served only to fuel my imagination as my mind's eye saw Leonard examining lofts and surveying the neighborhood. He was near, possibly peering through the window from the back seat of a Town Car as it rolled past clothing stores, cafes, delis, a subway stop, the Salvation Army, the Domino sugar factory. He was examining the landscape, beads of water sliding from the glass to the shiny black exterior of the car. These images sliced through my mind like sharp, piercing screams. Had he come to the conclusion that *all* Williamsburg residents were creatures of darkness and decay? Or was it just me? Did he believe that I was a perfect match for the side of his personality never seen by his Wall Street clients? Did he picture me in his harness?

The cold gray rain made me feel only more desolate.

***

It wasn't long after Leonard's trip to Brooklyn that he let his observations be known by updating his Yahoo! profile. It now featured a graphic close-up photo of a vagina tattooed with a fanged red devil, a shiny metal earring piercing the clitoris. He knew I would see it. He knew he had scared me so much I couldn't stop looking. On his new profile, below

a list of his favorite torture and rape websites was a taunting
poem:

Dear cousin, my cousin, Oh cousin so sweet.
I've seen where you live, I know what you eat.
I want to see your eyes when we first meet.

He was getting closer, I could feel it. He was emerging
from my email inbox, coming out into the real world, my
world. He was going to get a closer look at me, see me on
the street, go by my house, and run a finger along the gate.
And I had nowhere to go.

CHAPTER ONE

Information Not Released to the Public
Murderers are not monsters, they're men.
And that's the most frightening thing about them.
—Alice Sebold

After an hour of questioning and getting nowhere, one of the
detectives pulled out a photograph. He looked at it, placed
it on the table, and with his index finger, slid it toward me
across the metal desk. My heart constricted like a convulsion
of sharp pins. Fearing it might be a crime scene photo I
braced myself. But then I recognized it immediately, it was
a simple color photo of Jennifer Whipkey in life, one of two
images that I had seen in internet news reports about her
murder. Her beaming face seemed to hover ghostlike above
the cold steel desk, lying in front of me, looking at me. A
presence that was chillingly real. Her cheerful expression
was frozen in time. The atmosphere in the blue lit room felt

like a morgue. A mere one hundred pounds, she perished under a frenzy of sixty-three stab wounds.

Feeling helpless, I thought of her young child, motherless, like my nephew when my sister died. Death and sorrow—my uninvited twin companions, the feeling was always the same—my soul touching the third rail. I wondered what the detectives thought of me. They seemed like any other overworked cops following up on leads and hitting dead ends three years and counting. Could they really hold suspicions that I was connected to murder? Or were they hoping for just a shred of detail that could point them in the right direction and spring the case back to life? I told them that I felt horrible about her death, about the nature of this extremely violent crime, and how terrifying it must have been for her. That I had heartfelt sympathy for what her family was going through. I knew all about how the violent death of a young woman decimates the surviving family. My words felt futile. I wished that there something I could do to help them, but I knew nothing.

The meeting was long and unsettling. It was obvious they really wanted to solve this case which almost seemed personal for them. They had to answer to her family and her community. Their labor, frustration, and emotion were coming through in their questions about my life, my social life, how I came to know about Jennifer Whipkey's murder. The killing wasn't highly publicized outside of the small New Jersey Township of West Deptford. They wanted to know why I had information about a crime that wasn't made public. Of course it would draw the immediate attention of homicide detectives; that was completely understandable. But I was far removed from the terrifying deed and had only been pulled in by a net of lies as complex as a spider's web.

When it concluded, I thanked Special Agent Waller. I had the feeling I would be seeing him again very soon.

I was escorted to the elevator by another FBI official. I passed once again through multiple security checkpoints, each time fishing out ID from my wallet. All the while I reflected back in hopes of finding some sense in it all, while at the same point realizing that there are some things in this world that will never make any sense, things that you are forced to accept. Like actions with no reason or purpose, minds without conscience. In the thick glass that seemed to be everywhere, I caught a glimpse of my transparent reflection. It was still me, at least I looked the same, which surprised me as my life had been bluntly interrupted and thrown around like rag doll. I waved 'thanks' to the last security guard who buzzed me out and pushed through the revolving door. Out into the financial district, the city sunlight and street noise brought me back to normalcy. My town, New York City; ever moving along, never stopping, and reverberating in a million directions. It reinvigorated me.

It was a relief to re-join the ordinary world. I had emerged from the underworld, an 'other' realm, an unpretty world where bodies washed of their evidence are posed in caked puddles of blood. A world of chaos and order where square-shouldered law enforcement personnel dutifully knocked on doors, chased down witnesses, and presented evidence to prosecutors. Most of the time they wrapped up their cases, but tragically sometimes not, moving on to the next one in a ceaseless cycle of reward and frustration. I was left with the indelible knowledge that there were butcherers traveling the highways and lurking in back yards never to be found. Maybe even in my own backyard.

At the core of this saga is the reason I was here in the first place. This very strange thing that I had encountered had affected me in ways I could not have imagined. It had been almost two years since this all began in 2003, like a carnival of cracked mirrors with a quicksand floor with phantoms reflected in the distorted glass. I had to shake off these images and get back to my desk at Rizzoli International

Publications just a few stops away at 22nd Street and Park Avenue South. I had missed enough time already.

My life started out unsheltered, I was spared little in the bad old days of New York, but it was now all about books and publishers, authors, tours, media lists, and high expectations. A book publicist is essentially a salesman, a pitchman with an idea clutching a roster of ambitious authors and anxious editors. It's at times a waltz on a high wire, at others glamorous, yet bone-grinding hard work.

I hopped on the uptown subway immersed in a reel of thoughts of how I came to be exhaustively questioned by two New Jersey Homicide Detectives at One Federal Plaza, FBI Headquarters in New York City.

How did I get here? How did an otherwise normal everyday New Yorker who did not operate in the world of crime, wind up at FBI headquarters in downtown Manhattan now being vigorously interrogated about an unsolved brutal murder?

http://wbp.bz/softvoicea

Chapter 1

November 15, 1992

The meat locker bite of November winds chafed the flesh of the three rabbit hunters. Dreary skies cast a haunting fog through stark branches. The hunters were having no luck. An army of bunnies could nest beneath the slender trees, camouflaged amongst millions of windswept leaves.

DeMotte, Indiana police officer Kevin Jones, and his two neighbors, Bill Whitis and Terry Ward, kept a keen eye on the landscape that Sunday afternoon. Where there were rabbits, coyotes and wolves also roamed close by.

The rural wooded area, owned by a local woman named Mrs. McFarland, lay a mile from the interstate, one quarter mile west of County Line Road, and along a dirt path. The place was good for hunting but also frequented by daredevils on all-terrain vehicles. It was an illegal dumpsite too, as evidenced by aging appliances and outcast furniture.

Jones, Whitis, and Ward wended their way through naked tree limbs, marking the air with ghostly breaths. Then Jones spied what appeared to be a discarded mannequin about twenty yards away. The men stepped closer. Maybe not a mannequin? It looked so real. Maybe someone drugged or drunk? Possibly. There was a nudist colony a mere mile down the road.

The ivory limbs peeking through the leaves were no passed out nudist. This was a young woman, clearly dead. None of the men recognized her. There had been no recent reports in the area of a missing woman.

The body was that of a nude, slender white female. She appeared young, twenties or early thirties. Her pale skin wore a crust of fallen leaves and slivers of snow. One arm lay to her side, the other flopped across her abdomen.

Animals had come to sample the corpse, leaving nibble marks in the flesh on both feet, her upper right chest, and her left upper arm. Tan lines showed she had worn both a bikini and a one-piece swimsuit. Knobby knees projected from her slim legs. Her left ankle was adorned with two delicate gold chains: one plain, the other with three joined hearts.

Sexual assault was not likely, as evidenced by a tampon string dangling from her vagina.

Cold weather had slowed decomposition of the corpse. It would be difficult to identify the young woman. Her head and neck had been severed near the collarbone by some sort of serrated blade. It was not with the body.

As a police officer, Jones understood the need to preserve the crime scene. No one in his group touched the body or removed anything lying on or near it.

Officer Jones called for his friend Mr. Whitis "to run to my house and to notify the state police and to tell them what I had there and also there is an officer at the scene." He said, "It was probably a good hundred yards across the field to my house."

The call went out just after three p.m., but afternoon shadows had already begun to wisp through the lonely woods when Indiana state police investigators arrived. They lined up their vehicles along the dirt path and hiked about eighty feet through the woods to the crime scene.

An immediate search of the area turned up neither the victim's head nor a murder weapon. Soil samples were taken, but by five p.m., winter darkness blanketed any attempts to search further. A more thorough investigation would have to wait until the following day. Investigators hoped to identify the woman through the shriveled remnants of her fingerprints.

The leaves covering the body were collected, and then she was wrapped in a sheet and placed inside a body bag. Newton County Coroner Gerald A. Burman took the body to the Tippecanoe County Morgue in West Lafayette for autopsy.

The only potential evidence found was a piece of Styrofoam lying in the dirt beneath the corpse. A red rag hugged the ground fifty feet southeast of the site, and a piece of cloth lay seventy-five feet east. Investigators marked off the area with crime scene tape as darkness smothered the lonely saplings.

Investigators converged on the area the next morning to reexamine the slip of ground where the body had lain and to scour the surrounding area for clues. Indiana State Police Detective Sergeant William F. Krueger met with Detective Sergeant Richard Ludlow. Technicians called to the scene included Sergeant Rick Griswell, Sergeant Dave Kintzele, Gary Ekart, and Ken Buehrle.

The officers examined the area in a four hundred foot radius from the body's dumpsite. They combed an adjacent area containing items of trash for the missing head. The team also searched the sides of the field road and Jasper/Newton County Line Road. They found nothing but a silver and black PPG jacket in a ditch on the west side of County Line Road, about two hundred-fifty feet south of the dirt lane. The jacket did not appear to be evidence, but they collected it.

The young woman was no longer abandoned to the weather and the rats. Was she just another druggie, homeless and friendless? Surely she was someone's daughter, girlfriend, cousin, friend. The missing head could keep her nameless for years.

She would be easier to identify if anyone was actually looking for her.

Chapter 2

May 1992

The shock of the drive-by broke the peace of a perfect spring evening in Speedway, Indiana. The softball players stood on the field, open and defenseless. After a grueling and intense day at the Indianapolis Motor Speedway, members of the Marlboro-Penske team had escaped to a local park and challenged some other teams to a pickup game. Eager to unwind, drivers and mechanics were soon involved in the game, whooping and cheering the daring moves of team members and competitors alike.

A rented white cargo van swooped into the tidy small town park. The victims knew their attackers. The aggressors were three women who had tantalized them with a hot meal just hours before. Cynthia Albrecht, the thirty-one-year-old executive chef for Penske's Race Team, grinned with anticipation. Pretty and vivacious with blonde curls that bounced to her shoulders, Cindy exuded energy.

Cindy was joined by her best friends and partners in crime, Sandra Fink and Rebecca Miller. Cindy was the Penske Team's heartbeat, the personification of an enduring folk song. Sandi Fink, blonde and svelte, was their Barbie doll. Playful and stylish, she moved like soft rock. Jazzy little Becky Miller, the bright-eyed brunette, was quick and impromptu, always eager to swing into the next adventure.

As cooks for Penske, the three were acquainted with all the drivers, but they aimed their van toward Penske drivers Rick Mears and Emerson Fittipladi. Their crew chiefs Richard Buck and Rick Rinaman were also targeted. The assault came as a shock and everyone on the field began ducking and running — and laughing, as the three women pelted them with grapes, orange slices, kiwi, and strawberries.

"They loved it," Becky remembers. "We cleaned out the fruit basket that we stocked every day." Before any player could react, much less throw anything back, the three women sped away, cheering themselves for a successful drive-by fruiting.

"Did you see their faces?"

"We totally shocked them."

"Bet they can't make those moves in a race car."

Cindy, Sandi, and Becky were all married women whispering into their thirties but "acted like teenagers," Sandi says. "We were silly and goofy and bought each other underwear… it was a great time." And they danced with the thrill of being a part of IndyCar racing.

The race circuit was pure adrenaline. It had everything three young women could want: fast cars, excitement, travel. But most of all, the respect of their peers. Among Penske's IndyCar tribe, there was no pecking order. The hospitality team was held in no less esteem than drivers were. "We were family, all of us," Sandi says.

In the IndyCar community, team lines were fluid. If the women needed some tall guys with muscle to upright a tent, they only needed to ask. If Mary-Lin Murphy of Newman/Haas needed to borrow an ingredient, someone would gladly lend it.

Guests to the Penske hospitality tent included the cast of *90210* and George Harrison of Beatles fame. George made his way to the kitchen with his beautiful wife Olivia. Coffee was the hot beverage beneath the tent that day and the charming couple approached the cooks to ask for a cup of tea. Other VIPs included Donald Trump, General Norman Schwarzkopf, and Colonel Oliver North.

Food from the hospitality tent fueled much of the event, as no one had time to exit the track for a meal. No one wanted to leave anyway. The hospitality food could top the fare offered at any restaurant and it was plentiful enough to keep a hungry man hustling—no bologna sandwiches or limp noodle soup for these guys!

The parade of hot meals included Lobster Newburg, grilled blackened salmon with dill sauce, and southwest chicken with Mexican rice. Breakfast could include lox, caviar, omelets, and heart-shaped waffles with fresh fruit.

The Food Network channel had not yet been launched. If it had, Cindy could have starred on the channel as a gourmet chef. Her specialty was leg of lamb with fresh rosemary and mint. She had the talent to create her own sauces and dressings. The stylish Brazilian driver Emerson Fittipaldi liked to eat turkey on whole wheat with olive oil and red onion just before qualifying or racing. Cindy always made it just for him.

The three Penske hostesses were all married to IndyCar mechanics and met each other through their husbands. They traveled to all the races and made friends all over the country, but none of the events could top their hometown race, the Indianapolis 500, which is still the single biggest one-day sporting event in the world.

In 1992, Penske ran a three-car team, about fifty crewmembers. Another two hundred-fifty people, including sponsors, media, and special guests, were served at each meal. The hospitality tent buzzed like a school cafeteria. The service had to be fast, almost choreographed. Guests applauded the food as fabulous. Even on a budget, Cindy could dream up artistic meals which satisfied everyone from executives to famished mechanics.

The entire team embraced the Penske Way. In everything they did, their performance was to be exemplary. They were to be professional at all times. Presentation of the food first class. Most importantly, they were never, ever to run out of food.

Meals were cooked in a fourteen-foot trailer, its appliances and counters wedged in place with mathematical precision. Efficiency demanded the trailer carry all the cookware and service utensils needed to feed a variety of food to hundreds of people.

Penske hospitality was a team of five persons, the three hostesses and two men, working under the direction of Pete Twiddy. A born leader, Pete was the Marlboro side of Marlboro-Penske. In his trademark jeans and flip-flops, he was a bright-eyed and fluid guy on the beach, unhindered by his 6'8" height.

Canadian Glen Smith, tall and rugged, was Pete's right-hand man. He was humorous and ended his sentences with "eh." He was very protective of the women.

Smith and Bob Lawes, a British Adonis in short shorts, shared duties of transportation, setting up, and overseeing hospitality. Pete represented Marlboro while Lawes made sure the interests of the Penske family were respected. Working in sync, the five set up the awning, tables, chairs, and the buffet. "If we were on grass instead of concrete, we might lay down artificial grass to keep mud from guests' shoes," Lawes recalls.

All through the race they cooked, cleaned, and served and delivered food. Then they tore it all down and moved on to the next city on the race circuit. "Sometimes," Lawes recalls, "we'd be cleaning up a Sunday race and hurrying to get to the next race."

Each cook had assigned duties and a designated work area. Cindy created main courses, Sandi usually prepared desserts, while Becky was a sous chef, meaning she chopped tons of vegetables and juggled a myriad of other tasks.

From their trailer, the cooks could not see the race but they were very much a part of the excitement. The energy vibrated all over the Indianapolis Motor Speedway, and it was contagious.

Roger's rule was no alcohol would be served before the checkered flag, but once the race ended, Pete would say, "Make cocktails, girls. Make cocktails." They were also to keep champagne chilled and ready to pour in case a Penske driver won the race.

Becky says, "It was like Christmas every day, but very tiring." Although the race season only runs from April to October, the hospitality people who worked all the races were considered full time because the long hours over those frantic months equaled the hours a normal worker would log during a calendar year.

Bob Lawes says the schedule was nonstop. Sometimes they set out snacks for after the race and started tearing down to be off to the next race site by Tuesday. He recalls one weary morning when they were traveling to the track at five-thirty a.m.; Cindy was riding shotgun, singing cheerily with the radio. Bob, sitting in the back seat, asked who the song artist was. She told him and he said, "Well, why don't you let them sing it?"

Cindy turned, fuming, and smacked at him playfully. Bob says he can remember nothing but good times with Cindy, even though they were chronically exhausted and frequently under pressure.

Of course, they weren't the only team members racing the clock. Sometimes, Becky says, some driver or crewmember, due to car issues or other problems, would have no time to eat. They'd stand across the fence in Gasoline Alley and yell out, "Throw me a banana!" The women responded, flinging the fruit to their starving comrade or passing over a sandwich. The food was delivered with good wishes and the promise of more substantial fare later.

The trailer had no storage space and the women launched into the weekend running a grocery shopping marathon. "We'd trailer carts through the store," Sandi recalls, "and the bill would be, like, two thousand dollars."

Sandi's well-honed organizational skills enabled her to memorize the layout of all the grocery stores they used, from Pennsylvania to California. Cindy would hand the grocery list over to Sandi and have her organize it in the order of the aisles to save time.

Grocery shopping became an adventure in itself. First of all, the hospitality team was given thousands of dollars in cash to buy food at the beginning of the season. Becky says, "In May, that could be thirty thousand dollars, so we'd hide it in our pants, carry it inside our jackets, just stuff it all over the place, and act all innocent."

Cindy prowled the perishable departments, seeking ideas for tantalizing meals. She selected spices to blend into her own salad dressings. She bought packages of edible flowers and exotic vegetables that looked like they were fighting their way through puberty. Sandi describes Thumbelina baby carrots as "squirrelly-looking, stubby carrots with long strings on them." Cindy was horrified when Becky, while cleaning this alien produce, cut the strings off, but the women claim no one ever ate those carrots anyway.

Becky recalls that Cindy would eat anything, or at least try it. That would have been fine, except Cindy insisted her friends also try calamari, and cheese that smelled like an outhouse, and unpronounceable foods probably designed as torture by the CIA. Becky laughs, remembering, "If I wouldn't try something, she'd shove it in my mouth or just smear it on my face."

The cucumber game was Cindy's invention. When they shopped, she awarded the vegetable to whoever guessed closest to the register total. Becky claims Sandi always won, and usually guessed within ten dollars. "And she'd never guess an ordinary round number. She'd come up with some weird figure, like, $2,071.42, and she'd be maybe just a few dollars off."

The money was never really a game to Cindy. She kept careful watch over Penske's money. It was a matter of honor to her that the receipts and money matched to the penny. Between shopping trips, all the cash, including the loose change, stayed in a separate compartment in her travel bag.

On the way through the store, Sandi and Becky made a game of slipping items into Cindy's cart: adult diapers, feminine hygiene, dog treats, nasal spray… just any unexpected item that might startle her at the register. Now the women claim that when they're shopping, an odd item will simply fall off the shelf in front of them. They say it happens a lot. "And we'll be like, hi, Cindy!"

Whether shopping, working, or just being together, the trio had spontaneous fun. But not everyone was laughing with them.

http://wbp.bz/rtja

CHAPTER ONE

SGT. MICHAEL CROOKE GOES TO MIDTOWN MENTAL HEALTH

Michael Crooke joined the Indianapolis Police Department in the late 1960s. By 1994, he had pretty much seen and heard it all. He had done his time on the streets in various divisions and worked his way up to the prestigious homicide unit. Despite the importance of the work done there, the unit was located in a large cluster of rooms with most of the desks pushed up against each other, little natural light, and no decoration of any kind. Metal desks, metal chairs, black telephones, grungy-looking printers, and fax machines.

He was at his desk in the unit on January 7, 1994, when a uniformed IPD officer entered the unit to report an unusual situation to the detective in charge. Crooke listened as Officer Frank Ingram described what he had just learned about a Michelle Engron Jones. It would be the beginning of more than two years of investigation, working leads, literally digging the earth, pressing for the truth, and ultimately charging Jones for the murder of her four-year-old son Brandon.

Officer Ingram told Sgt. Crooke that he had been dispatched to Midtown Mental Health, which was a unit of the county hospital known as Wishard. It's not unusual for an officer to be sent to Midtown to investigate the cause of a hospitalization, especially if the patient claims to have been abused, assaulted, or is self-harming. When he arrived, Ingram met with Toni Goffredo, a clinical crisis counselor, who had interviewed Jones when she appeared at the facility earlier in the day. Goffredo told Ingram that Jones checked in due to "stress" caused by taking her deceased child, dropping him off somewhere, and failing to have a proper burial for the child.

What on Earth? These statements could be the vivid imagination of a mentally disturbed woman, describe an accidental death, abandonment, or an intentional killing. Crooke immediately returned to Midtown with Ingram but learned that Jones had been heavily sedated and was unable to meet with law enforcement.

Three days later, Sgt. Crooke spoke with Jones' social worker at Midtown. The social worker told Crooke that Jones was able to coherently describe what had happened and invited Crooke to come meet with her. They arranged for an interview on January 13, 1994. By then, Jones had been in the unit for nearly a week and had received several visitors.

Crooke, dressed in plain clothes but having identified himself as a detective, met with Michelle Jones in a room designated by the floor nurse. The nurse led Crooke into a small conference room and brought Jones into the room. She told Crooke that she wanted to be called by her maiden name, Engron. She explained that she gave birth to a boy on November 11, 1987. She told Crooke that she named him Brandon Lamarr Sims and that the father was Kevin Sims.

Jones appeared to understand all of Crooke's questions and gave coherent and accurate (when later confirmed) answers to most of his questions. She volunteered much of what she told him, including that she and Brandon had lived at the Georgetown Apartments at the time of his death. She was articulate and seemed high functioning.

Crooke would later quote much of what she told him that day in an affidavit in support of her arrest:

Michelle Engron Jones said that two years prior (1992) she was taking large doses of medication and drugs. She left her son at home, unattended, for approximately one week. She thought this was in July or August of 1992. When she returned home, the child was dead. She placed him in her vehicle and drove to police headquarters to report the death. Because of her religious beliefs at that time she felt a lack of trust for people of the white race. When she arrived at police headquarters she only saw white people. She left and went to a cemetery where she was going to bury him, but no one was there. She drove north on I-65 to what she believed was the Attica exit. Somewhere near that exit, she placed the body at the bottom of an embankment. She said she was sure she could take us to the location of the body.

Crooke would later relate that she never referred to the child by his name. He tried to comprehend the detachment he observed. It seemed to him that Jones was more concerned about what her friends thought of her than the absence of her son.

Crooke told Jones that he wanted her to take him to find Brandon's body. She agreed, saying that she was willing to do so. Crooke made arrangements to meet so that she could direct him to the area where she claimed to have put Brandon's body. When he returned to Midtown, Jones advised him, through the floor nurse, that she had hired a lawyer, Mark Earnest. She refused to speak to Crooke and did not take him to Brandon's body. Michelle Engron Jones was twenty-one years old.

CHAPTER TWO

A NEEDLE IN A HAYSTACK

Crooke returned to the unit believing that something had happened to Brandon Sims. But would he ever be able to prove it? Was there even a child named Brandon Sims? Without a body, it would be nearly impossible to prove that the child was dead. Besides that, Crooke had to convince himself that Brandon was a real, live child. Then he had to figure out if the child was dead. And then he would have to learn how the child died.

Was Jones hiding the child from his father? Was the child staying with relatives? Had she sold the child? Crooke needed to know a lot more about Brandon Sims.

Within twenty-four hours of his first meeting with Michelle Jones, Sgt. Crooke located and met with Kevin Sims and Arlene Blevins. Kevin told Crooke that he and Arlene had been searching for Brandon for months. They provided a well-worn photograph of Kevin and his son. Crooke saw a pudgy, smiling toddler in the arms of Kevin. Both were grinning and pointing, relaxed and happy. He learned that the photograph was taken while Arlene was caring for Brandon, before she had returned him to his mother.

Kevin and his mother gave tape-recorded statements to Crooke. They wanted Brandon back. Crooke did not share what Jones had told him.

How could he tell these family members that Brandon was dead when he didn't know if it was true? He just couldn't be sure. Was Michelle Jones credible? Crooke decided that the child was, at the least, missing. He filed a missing person report with that unit of IPD. He needed help looking for and finding Brandon Sims. Maybe the child would be found alive. Maybe.

On January 27, 1994, Sgt. Crooke gathered police resources to search for Brandon Sims. This would prove to be the first of many attempts by the Indianapolis Police Department to locate Brandon if he was indeed dead. Crooke and Lt. Mark Rice met with the Indiana State Police at the Attica exit off I-65 to try to find little Brandon's body. It was freezing cold in Indiana but a group of officers, detectives, and troopers (some on their own time as volunteers) searched for baby Brandon Sims.

They searched the woods surrounding the exit and on-ramps of the Attica exit on I-65 and the surrounding area.

They dug up any ground that looked like it had been disturbed. They tried to identify children's clothing or blankets that may have been left or buried with Brandon, since parents who killed their children, especially a young child, were known to wrap the body in the child's favorite blankets, leave their stuffed animals or some other comforting item from the child's life with the body. The officers spent hours looking for a body. They found nothing.

There are thirty-one exits on I-65 heading toward Chicago from the I-465 northern loop of Indianapolis. The Attica exit, onto State Road 28, is the eighth. Crooke wondered why Jones would have chosen the Attica exit. He found no connection between her and Attica. It was not particularly isolated or wooded. Was this really where she left Brandon's body? Although it had been a while since he died, evidence of his body should have remained if it was "laid" or buried there as she had told him.

Frustrated, Crooke searched the records for unidentified bodies that may have been found in the area for the preceding three years. There were no bodies found. It was becoming a mystery that haunted him. A four year old left alone in life and, if Jones was to be believed, in death.

So Crooke dug in. He was determined to find out what had happened to the smiling toddler from the photograph. He tracked down a birth certificate proving that Brandon Lamarr Sims had been born to Michelle Engron and Kevin Sims. He obtained Brandon's medical records from Wishard Hospital where Brandon had been born and Riley Children's Hospital where Brandon had been seen by pediatricians. He located welfare records for Brandon and even obtained the birth announcement that Arlene Blevins had saved. He knew that Brandon was a real child, not the figment of Jones' imagination.

All the while, Michelle Jones, who had left Midtown, was back to her life. No charges had been filed against her. She continued working, dancing, dating, and living with friends. Crooke knew little about her but was bound and determined to know everything he could about this seemingly dispassionate woman who had abandoned her child.

Crooke tracked down Mae Engron, Michelle's mother. Mae was brusque. She had been injured while working for the US Postal Service and had been living on disability for years. She had not had any contact with her daughter since she was placed in the group home, nearly eight years earlier. Mae gave Crooke names and contact information for other members of the family. Crooke methodically tracked each down, but Jones had lost touch or not been in contact for years. Her family knew that Brandon had been born but had no idea where he was. No one had seen him in more than two years.

Crooke continued searching for evidence. Months went by. No child's body had been uncovered. Michelle Engron Jones had "lawyered up" and was not going to speak with the police or anyone else about the case. Despite her earlier admission, she resumed her life as if nothing had happened to her only child. She returned to work at Eli Lilly. Kevin and Arlene were becoming increasingly frantic to find Brandon. Crooke was getting nowhere.

http://wbp.bz/iga

 WILDBLUE PRESS

See even more at:
http://wbp.bz/tc

More True Crime You'll Love From WildBlue Press

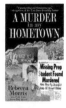

A MURDER IN MY HOMETOWN by Rebecca Morris

Nearly 50 years after the murder of seventeen year old Dick Kitchel, Rebecca Morris returned to her hometown to write about how the murder changed a town, a school, and the lives of his friends.

wbp.bz/hometowna

THE BEAST I LOVED by Robert Davidson

Robert Davidson again demonstrates that he is a master of psychological horror in this riveting and hypnotic story ... I was so enthralled that I finished the book in a single sitting. "—James Byron Huggins, International Bestselling Author of The Reckoning

wbp.bz/tbila

BULLIED TO DEATH by Judith A. Yates

On September 5, 2015, in a public park in LaVergne, Tennessee, fourteen-year-old Sherokee Harriman drove a kitchen knife into her stomach as other teens watched in horror. Despite attempts to save her, the girl died, and the coroner ruled it a "suicide." But was it? Or was it a crime perpetuated by other teens who had bullied her?

wbp.bz/btda

SUMMARY EXECUTION by Michael Withey

"An incredible true story that reads like an international crime thriller peopled with assassins, political activists, shady FBI informants, murdered witnesses, a tenacious attorney, and a murderous foreign dictator."—Steve Jackson, New York Times bestselling author of NO STONE UNTURNED

wbp.bz/sea

58588674R00150

Made in the USA
Middletown, DE
08 August 2019